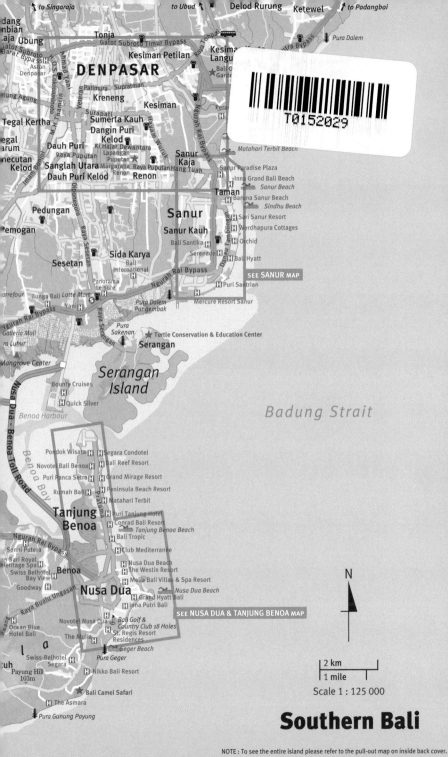

to Singaraja ↑   to Ubud ↑   Delod Rurung   Ketewel   ↑ to Padangbai

dang
nbian
aja Ubung
Barat
Barat Bypass
Aston
Denpasar

Tonja
Gatot Subroto Timur Bypass
Kesiman Petilan
Kesima
Langu
Bali O
Garde
Pura Dalem

DENPASAR

nung Agung
Patimura Supratman
Kreneng
Kesiman

Tegal Kertha
Surapati
Sumerta Kauh
Dangin Puri
Kelod
Ki Hajar Dewantara

egal
arum
Dauh Puri
Raya Puputan
Lapangan
Puputan
Renon
Sanur
Kaja

necutan
Kelod
Sanglah Utara
Dauh Puri Kelod
Margarana
Renon
Raya Puputan
Hang Tuah

Matahari Terbit Beach

Sanur Paradise Plaza
Inna Grand Bali Beach
Sanur
Sanur Beach
Baruna Sanur Beach
Sindhu Beach
Taman
Sari Sanur Resort
Werdhapura Cottages
Orchid
Bali Hyatt

Pedungan
Pemogan

Sanur
Sanur Kauh
Bali Santika
Serenade

Sida Karya
Bali
International
Panorama
Leisure

Sesetan

SEE **SANUR** MAP

rrefour
Bunga Bali Lotte Mart
Yani
Ngurah Rai Bypass
Puri Santrian
Mercure Resort Sanur

Pura Dalem
Pangembak

Galleria Mall
ra Luhur

Pura
Sakenan
★ Turtle Conservation & Education Center

Mangrove Center
Serangan

Bounty Cruises
Quick Silver

Serangan
Island

Badung Strait

Benoa Harbour

Benoa Bay

Pondok Wisata
Segara Condotel
Novotel Bali Benoa
Bali Reef Resort
Puri Panca Setra
Grand Mirage Resort
Rumah Bali
Peninsula Beach Resort
Matahari Terbit

Tanjung Benoa
Puri Tanjung Hotel
Conrad Bali Resort
Tanjung Benoa Beach
Bali Tropic
Ngurah Rai Bypass
Club Mediterranee

Sonni Putera
Sari Royal
Heritage Spa
Swiss Belhotel
Bay View
Goodway
Benoa
Nusa Dua Beach
The Westin Resort
Melia Bali Villas & Spa Resort

Nusa Dua
Raya Bualu Ungasan
Nusa Dua Beach
Grand Hyatt Bali
Inna Putri Bali

Ocean Blue
Hotel Bali
Novotel Nusa Dua
Bali Golf &
Country Club 18 Holes
St. Regis Resort
Residences

SEE **NUSA DUA & TANJUNG BENOA** MAP

Swiss-Belhotel
Segara
Geger Beach
Pura Geger
The Mulia

uh
Payung Hill
103m
Nikko Bali Resort

Bali Camel Safari

The Asmara
Pura Gunung Payung

N

2 km
1 mile
Scale 1 : 125 000

Southern Bali

NOTE : To see the entire island please refer to the pull-out map on inside back cover.

Paul Greenway is physically based in Adelaide, South Australia, but emotionally, mentally, and spiritually he resides in Indonesia, particularly Bali. He wrote over 30 guidebooks for Lonely Planet, including about Bali, Lombok, and Indonesia; lived in Jakarta for years, from where he taught students and trained teachers across the region; studied Indonesian in Bali and other provinces; and taught Indonesian at Australian high schools. Paul has also traveled extensively throughout the archipelago from—as the nationalistic song goes—"Sabang to Merauke." During the rare times he's not traveling, living, or working in Bali, he's trying to concoct some reason to go back there. Paul´s first novel, *Bali & Oates* (based you know where) has recently been published. More details are available through www.paulgreenway.net.

Paul Greenway

Published by Tuttle Publishing, an imprint of Periplus Editions (HK) Ltd

www.tuttlepublishing.com

Copyright © 2014 Periplus Editions (HK) Ltd

ISBN: 978-0-8048-4211-2

Distributed by

North America, Latin America & Europe
Tuttle Publishing
364 Innovation Drive
North Clarendon, VT 05759-9436 U.S.A.
Tel: 1 (802) 773-8930
Fax: 1 (802) 773-6993
info@tuttlepublishing.com
www.tuttlepublishing.com

Japan
Tuttle Publishing
Yaekari Building, 3rd Floor
5-4-12 Osaki
Shinagawa-ku
Tokyo 141-0032
Tel: (81) 3 5437-0171
Fax: (81) 3 5437-0755
sales@tuttle.co.jp
www.tuttle.co.jp

Asia Pacific
Berkeley Books Pte. Ltd.
61 Tai Seng Avenue, #02-12
Singapore 534167
Tel: (65) 6280-1330
Fax: (65) 6280-6290
inquiries@periplus.com.sg
www.periplus.com

17 16 15 14   5 4 3 2 1

Printed in Singapore   1312CP

TUTTLE TRAVEL PACK

Bali
& Lombok

Paul Greenway

TUTTLE Publishing

Tokyo | Rutland, Vermont | Singapore

PARADISE BECKONS

Bali is many things to many people. To some, the attractions are the sun, sea and shopping, and the never-ending search for The Happiest Hour. Many admire the variety of landscapes while hiking around volcanoes, whirling across lakes on speedboats, and rafting down rivers. And others prefer Bali's cultural riches, seeking spiritual enlightenment from visiting temples and attending yoga retreats. In fact, it's possible to attend a majestic Hindu ceremony at a 1,000-year-old temple in eastern Bali in the morning, walk around a volcanic lake during the afternoon, watch the dripping sunset at Tanah Lot and finish up at a Seminyak nightclub as trendy as anything in Europe. But Bali is somewhere to dawdle, not run; a place to linger and relish its distinctive sights, sounds, and tastes.

The unique, ancient culture and religion that dominates every aspect of Balinese life remarkably somehow survives and even co-exists with the malls, resorts, and nightclubs that tourism and modernism has brought. Unshakeable values regarding family and village ensure that faith, traditions, and rituals have rarely changed for centuries, yet allow for inevitable modern intrusions. The Balinese are blessed and they know it, as they constantly give thanks to the gods for the climate and topography that allow them to be self-sufficient, while relishing a life on one of the most glorious places on earth.

The Balinese have always resisted intrusion and repelled invasion, whether from Islam during the 16th century or interference by Jakarta since independence; even many of the Dutch colonialists could see the benefits of preserving rather than destroying Balinese culture. But rampant development continues and is now more relentless than ever as tourists—foreign and Indonesian—arrive with insatiable needs from finite resources. As more rice fields disappear to build bungalows for foreigners, Bali may soon reach its zenith; maybe, it already has become a "Paradise Lost." But the pessimists have been saying that ever since the 1930s, when an average of three westerners arrived per day.

Although nearby, and with a similar landscape of rice fields, volcanoes, and surfing beaches, Lombok is vastly different in numerous ways, most notably because the dominant religion is Islam, not Hinduism, and the indigenous people are Sasak. Consequently, ceremonies are infrequent and traditions and cultures less obvious, but the people are also warm and inviting. Tourism flourishes at Senggigi, the Gili Islands, and Kuta beach to the south, but not (yet) in the un-abated and unabashed ways found on Bali. Yet, ironically, more and more tourists are finding out that a primary attraction of Lombok is the lack of other tourists.

CONTENTS

Bali & Lombok at a Glance

Geography Located along the southern edge of the Indonesian archipelago, Bali is dominated by a series of cloud-piercing volcanoes along which villages cling to the fertile soil and create amphitheaters of rice fields cascading down the rain-soaked slopes. The tallest, most volatile and, therefore, most revered volcano is Gunung Agung (3,142m/10,308ft). The coast is lined with cliffs, mangroves and beaches, while the Taman Nasional Bali Barat national park protects virgin rainforests in the far west. Lombok is slightly smaller than Bali and with a similar landscape, but dominated by one volcano: Gunung Rinjani (3,726m/12,224ft), the second-highest peak in the country.

Climate Only a few degrees (and 375km/233 miles) south of the equator, Bali and Lombok are tropical, not monsoonal. There's a definite wet season (October to March) and dry season (April to September), but it may still rain during the "dry" and not rain for a week in the "wet;" and it usually comes down in short blasts, often late in the afternoon or evening. The mountainous landscapes ensure that precipitation is often localized, so it may, for example, be flooding in Ubud but dry 25km (40 miles) away in Sanur. The weather shouldn't affect your travel plans, but the peak seasons may (see page 117).

People Bali's population of some four million almost doubles every year with tourists. Although a large percentage live in the capital Denpasar, the second-largest city, Singaraja, and the southern tourist areas, most Balinese still follow a lifestyle

dominated by village concepts of communal sharing and order. This is most evident in the *subak* system of shared irrigation for rice fields and the *bale banjar* meeting hall where societal decisions are made by elders. The indigenous Sasak people of Lombok are Muslims, although some 100,000 of the island's population of three million are Hindu. People on both islands still prefer to live with their extended families in large compounds, with segregated areas for working, sleeping, and praying, and a small *bale* pavilion for meeting guests.

Language Indonesian is the language of instruction in schools and in government, and used extensively by the inhabitants of Bali and Lombok. Most Balinese also proudly speak *bahasa Bali*, a different, complex language, but the unique script is rarely used. On Lombok, many locals converse in *bahasa Sasak*, which is an oral, not written, language. English is taught at school and widely used in tourist centers, but a short detour and you may need to use a little *Bahasa Indonesia* (see page 124).

Religion It's impossible to overstate the importance of religion in Balinese life. The form of Hinduism which 92 percent of the island follows was imported from India, via Java, some 1,000 years ago but is now distinct. Religion encompasses every element of Balinese life: shrines are found in every home and hotel, and shops and streets often strewn with *canang* trays made from palm leaves and filled with offerings of rice and flowers. Some people, especially around Candikuning and the west, originate from Java, Lombok, and other islands and practice Islam. While Hinduism still thrives along the western coast, the majority of Lombok is Islamic. Some in the north follow the unofficial Wektu Telu sect, which combines Islam with Hinduism, Buddhism, and animist beliefs, although adherents are officially classified as Muslims.

Culture Balinese culture permeates every pore of society and is as much an attraction to some visitors as the sun, surf, and shops. Despite encroaching modernism and tourist-led hedonism, Balinese still embrace a unique spiritual faith and omnipresent culture not seen anywhere else on earth. Everything has a purpose and deep meaning, primarily aimed at appeasing the gods to ensure a happy life, healthy family and abundant harvest. Private lives are part of communal law under the guidance and authority of the *banjar* association (mostly of married men), and cremations are as elaborate as anything celebrated during a person's life.

On Lombok, the family and village are also paramount to indigenous Sasak culture, and traditional customs and laws regulate an individual's life. Almost all Sasaks are Muslims, so the mosque is the dominant force, but ceremonies are less significant and traditions less public.

Arts & Crafts Bali's artistic prowess is no more evident than in Ubud, where galleries galore sell all sorts of paintings and carvings that incorporate the island's landscape, mythology and, of course, religion. Popular crafts, such as *batik* cloth and *songket* weaving, and the unusual form of *gerebah* pottery still practiced around Lombok, are explained in the Quick Guide to Handicrafts & Arts (see page 89).

Architecture From the moment you arrive, you'll be struck by Bali's unique architectural designs and marvel at the skills involved in carving the symbols of demons and gods that decorate gates, pillars, and roofs to protect inhabitants from evil invaders. Temples, homes and, indeed, entire villages are designed to face downstream towards the sea (*kelod*) or the mountains (*kaja*), which are home to the gods.

Tuttle Travel Pack Bali & Lombok
HOW TO USE THIS BOOK

Full of up-to-date, thoroughly researched information by people who have lived, studied, and worked in the country, the Tuttle series of Travel Packs are indispensable companions on your global travels. The portable size and straightforward format always makes them easy to use, no matter if you're a regular or first-time visitor.

At the front of this book we provide an overview, including the geography, climate, and people of Bali and Lombok and, importantly, the unique culture, crafts, and architecture of both islands.

Chapter 1 lists the 21 Best Sights across Bali and Lombok, including the most alluring beaches, the most resplendent temples, and the greatest outdoor activities like cycling and snorkeling, as well as other highlights, popular or lesser-known. To help you plan your stay, the Making the Most of Your Visit section offers advice about where to base yourself and how to make those "tough" decisions about what to see and do among the myriad of attractions based on your preferred interests and level of comfort.

In Chapter 2, we detail a number of daily excursions across Bali, from the hedonistic southern beaches to the northern and eastern coasts, and the cultural and volcanic heartlands in between. We focus on places that are well-known and popular, such as Ubud, Sanur, and Lovina, but also lakeside temples, traditional villages, and undeveloped beaches that tourists rarely visit or even know about. We also include Bali's sister island, Lombok, which is similar in some ways but vastly different in others, and doesn't have the obvious trappings of mass tourism: pollution, urban sprawl, and high prices.

A vital part of this book is Chapter 3 in which the author offers many personal recommendations. From his vast experience of traveling, working, and studying in Bali and Lombok, he provides a list of the best of the best for both islands, including the grandest and most unique hotels, from budget to luxury and in between, and premium places to dine, whether it's on a beach or among the chaos of Kuta. Kids, night-clubbers, shopaholics, and outdoor enthusiasts are certainly not forgotten either, with special sections dedicated to the very best of what Bali and Lombok have to offer.

Lastly, the Travel Facts section provides everything you need to be aware of, including must-knows like visas and money, explanations about health and events, some basic Indonesian to help you make the most of your visit, and details about how to get there and travel around.

No guidebook is complete without detailed maps, however, so we provide dozens of maps, as well as a large double-sided, pull-out map of Bali and Lombok based on an updated version of Periplus' renowned series of maps.

While information was correct at the time of printing, places on both islands do sometimes close, change owners, or fall in quality. The publisher cannot accept responsibility for any errors that may be contained in this Travel Pack, but we also encourage readers to contact us with corrections and recommendations.

CHAPTER 1
BALI & LOMBOK'S
Best Sights

Some rarely venture outside the confines of their chosen resort area, but Bali and Lombok offer almost every conceivable attraction from temples on volcanic slopes in Bali's central highlands to hot springs among tropical forests to the north, as well as quaint villages clinging to Indonesia's second-highest peak, Mount Rinjani, on Lombok. Online research, or a visit to any travel agency, will quickly confirm the overwhelming number of things to do and places to go and see, which is why we've done the hard work for you and compiled a list of 21 Best Sights across both islands. Including sunset dinners at beachside cafés, hypnotic dances at cliff-top temples, and cycling around a care-free (and car-free) island, make sure you cross as many as possible off this list.

1 Tanah Lot Temple
2 Lake Bratan, Bedugul Highlands
3 Jimbaran Beach Seafood Dinner
4 Padangbai Village, East Bali
5 Ulu Watu Temple, South Bali
6 Pasir Putih Beach, East Bali
7 Tirtagangga Water Palace
8 Cycling on Nusa Lembongan Island
9 Ubud's Taman Saraswati Dances
10 Rice Terraces at Jatiluwih
11 Ubud's Monkey Forest
12 Gunung Kawi Rock Temples
13 Banjar Village, North Bali
14 Mount Batur Natural Hot Springs
15 From Ujung to Amed, East Bali
16 Snorkeling Lombok's Gili Islands
17 Southern Lombok's Kuta Beach
18 Lombok's Senaru Village
19 Pura Lingsar Temple in Lombok
20 Lombok's Senggigi Beach
21 Taman Narmada Gardens, Lombok

Making the Most of Your Visit

You obviously know the limits of your time and budget, but we can help you choose a base. Bali and Lombok are compact, so while it is possible to day trip from one place to another, traffic, poor roads, and mountainous terrain will seriously affect traveling times. While finding a quiet, remote base with few tourists sounds tempting, hotels will have cold water and, maybe, squat toilets; menus may be limited to only rice and noodles; and you'll probably need to rely on jam-packed public transport. Buses and mini-vans called *bemo* cater exclusively for locals, so they travel to non-tourist hubs like Denpasar and Gianyar, while services are, for example, poor in Ubud and non-existent for Kuta. So, base yourself in locations that have the wide range of facilities you want, the sort of transport you need, and the type of places you wish to visit.

Bali: The overwhelming majority of people base themselves near the southern beaches or Ubud, which means that vast areas, including tourist centers along the east and north coast and the smaller islands, are comparatively quiet; even more so during the low season. If you're mostly interested in shopping, surfing and clubbing, Kuta is popular, although its claustrophobic lanes and traffic-clogged roads may not appeal to kids and mature-aged visitors. For what Kuta has to offer, but with more space and fewer people, head to the adjacent beaches of Tuban (also known as South Kuta) and Legian, or to Seminyak for a little more sophistication.

Sanur has no waves—and, therefore, no surfers—and limited nightlife, but certainly has more than enough tourist facilities to satisfy most, and it is the departure point for the charming island of Nusa Lembongan. Further around the southern peninsula is Nusa Dua, a gated zone of four- and five-star resorts where guests rarely want (or need) to venture far from their vast hotel complexes. To the north, Tanjung Benoa is a more affordable version of Nusa Dua and the center for water sports.

Ubud is the undoubted cultural and spiritual heartland of Bali and also geographically convenient for day trips to the beaches in the south and east, and the numerous temples, villages, lakes, and volcanoes of central Bali. Also, Ubud is cooler and cheaper than the southern resorts. The east coast, which is increasingly popular as it becomes more accessible, offers quiet beaches, un-touristy villages, and revered temples. The major east coast bases are Padangbai, a jumping off point for speedboats to the Gili Islands and ferries to Lombok, but also a charming village in itself; and Candidasa, which is a beach resort without much beach. Further along the east coast, Amed is an extended collection of laidback fishing villages with rocky, gray beaches unsuitable for swimming, but excellent for underwater exploration. Similarly, along the northern coast, Lovina is spread over many kilometers, and while the beaches are unattractive many love the village atmosphere and numerous attractions nearby.

Lombok: Facilities across the strait in the tourist centers of Senggigi, the Gili Islands, and Lombok's own Kuta beach are as good (but not as numerous) as Bali, but the range of transport, hotels, and restaurants is far more limited elsewhere and often caters for Indonesians, not western tourists. Senggigi is a perfect base: a likable beach resort close enough to explore western Lombok. Many zip across to the Gilis from Bali and never set foot on Lombok, which is a shame. Adorable and astoundingly undeveloped, Kuta is an increasingly popular holiday destination and base from which to discover the rugged southern coast.

1 Tanah Lot Temple
Sunset, cliff-top dining, temples and... touristy crowds

Tanah Lot is unquestionably one of the most visited places on Bali—by tourists for its dramatic setting, and by Hindus as one of six revered, cardinal temples. Built some 500 years ago by a Javanese priest and dedicated to the Goddess of the Sea, Tanah Lot seems more dedicated these days to the God of Souvenir Stalls. But it's all about the location, especially at sunset; the temple itself is 100m (320ft) offshore and only accessible to Hindus, and unreachable by anyone at high tide. The cliff-side path to the north passes the **Pura Enjung Galuh** temple (behind which are the best views of Tanah Lot), then some steps down to a wave-swept beach, and later to **Pura Batu Bolong** temple perched atop another rocky headland. Continuing to a clearing where a spectacular *Kecak* dance is held every evening after sunset (6.30pm; 45 mins), the path finishes at the recommended **Melasti Tanah Lot** restaurant (see page 82). The path south of Tanah Lot weaves through a handful of **eateries** (set up for sunset drinks and meals, but open all day) and ends at the **Pan Pacific Nirwana Bali Resort** and golf course, controversially built higher than the temple. To avoid the hordes, come during the day; in fact, before 9am you may have the whole complex to yourself. Visiting during the day allows you more time to admire impressive *padi* fields along the way and detour to rugged beaches such as **Pantai Seseh**. Traveling with your own transport is *not* recommended: roads are poorly-signed and traffic is reminiscent of a football final. Join an organized tour or take a taxi (which will wait).

Times Daily 7am–7pm **Dress** As you wish (you can't enter) **Getting There** From Seminyak, turn left to "Canggu/Tabanan" and follow the signs. Public transport from Denpasar is limited and not available after sunset. **Tip** Inside the complex are two mid-priced hotels, while Astiti Graha homestay is 500m (546yds) before the entrance **Also nearby** Taman Ayun temple at Mengwi

2 Lake Bratan, Bedugul Highlands
Speedboats and seafood; tourism Indonesian-style

One of Bali's most underrated attractions, the gorgeous volcanic lake of Danau Bratan (Beratan) is incredibly popular with Indonesian tourists but surprisingly ignored by foreigners. While many understandably visit the striking **Pura Ulun Danu Bratan** temple, there's much more to see and do at the southern edge of the lake. **Taman Rekreasi Bedugul** (Bedugul Recreation Park) is one of the best places on Bali for water sports such as canoes, banana boating, parasailing, and jet-skiing—and without the waves and high prices found along the southern beaches. The obligatory **souvenir shops** sell different brands of tacky stuff to Kuta, and at fixed prices designed for Indonesian (not western) tourists; and just as mandatory is the tiny **temple** (closed) at the western end surrounded by pesky monkeys. A **walking path** which starts opposite the fruit stalls skirts the lake and heads along a ridge to the top of Mount Mangu (2,020m/6,627ft), a six hour return hike. Opposite the turn-off to the park, **The**

Strawberry Hill Resort (0368-21265) can arrange guides for **hikes** to nearby waterfalls and vanilla plantations, and around Buyan and Tamblingan lakes. Most visitors to Bedugul take a 15 minute whirl around the lake on a **speedboat** passing upmarket villas, farms growing an unpalatable combination of strawberries and garlic and, of course, that famous temple. Then they settle down to lunch at the **restaurant** (see page 83) overlooking the lake and under the towering volcanoes. But what makes Bedugul *really* special is that it caters exclusively for Indonesian tourists, so on weekends and public holidays the place is packed and perfect for watching Indonesians enjoying themselves—a great spectacle itself; while at other times the lake and park are eerily empty.

Times Daily 9am-8pm **Address** Turn-off is 1km (0.62 miles) down from Candikuning, then another 300m (328yds) to the entrance **Getting There** Public transport between Denpasar and Lovina; or shuttle bus between the southern beaches and Lovina **Also nearby** Jatiluwih rice terraces

3 Jimbaran Beach Seafood Dinner
Sunset, candles, fireworks, and serenading buskers

Despite its magnificent beach and proximity to Kuta and the airport, Jimbaran remains surprisingly undeveloped. This relative tranquillity is shattered, however, every day from 5pm when crowds rush there for the famed combination of seafood, beer, beach, sunset and more beer. During the afternoon, much of the long, curved stretch of white sand is set up with masses of tables. An extraordinary array of fish, lobster, prawns, and squid are available, although the days of cooking on the beach using traditional grills fired by coconut husks are long gone; meals are now prepared en masse in the back kitchen. Seafood is priced by the 100g or kilogram and should (but check) include rice, vegetables, sauce—such as garlic, sweet and sour, or *bumbu Bali* (Balinese spices)—and a fruit platter. Your culinary delights may then be enriched further by post-sunset entertainment including fireworks, *Legong* dances and parading musicians. Most restaurants offer similar meals, prices, service and setting, and are lumped together in four locations. (1) The southern **Muaya Beach Café Area** is quieter and closer to the resorts. (2) The cluster at the end of

Jalan Pemelisan Agung is the most scenic and accessible by public transport. (3) The northern end at **Kedonganan** is where tour groups head so it's always packed, but restaurants are more likely to offer wine, entertainment, and a Plan B if it rains. (4) Further north, the cafés along Kelan Beach are cheaper, with the added attraction of watching planes slide along the runway. Consider coming earlier than 5pm or even staying the whole day (see page 36).

Times Restaurants open daily 11am–9pm
Getting There Organized tours (including food, transport, but not drinks); by taxi (which will wait, or get another afterwards); or infrequent *bemo* from southern Tuban (but not after dark) **Tips** Over-charging is not uncommon: check the price and weight of seafood before ordering; ensure there are no hidden extras (other than tax); and double-check your bill **Also nearby** Ulu Watu temple and Garuda Wisnu Kencana Cultural Park

4 Padangbai Village, East Bali
This sheltered bay along the east coast is a delight

This compact and unpretentious village nestled along a scenic cove is often ignored, but Padangbai is much more than a departure point for ferries to Lombok and speedboats to the Gili Islands: it's also a very appealing base from which to explore the east coast. Padangbai offers zero nightlife and even less shopping, but that's part of the attraction; and the ferry terminal is surprisingly unobtrusive—except for the horn-happy boat captains who delight in interrupting the serenity every hour, day and night. From the fork at the end of the main street, a path (200m/218yds) heads right at Topi Inn and finishes at the revered, millennium-old **Pura Silayukti** temple, regularly used for massive ceremonies. Steps down the other side of the headland lead to a cliff-side shrine with dramatic views towards Candidasa. The village **beach** is lined with *jukung* fishing boats and superb for photos, but less ideal for **swimming**. There are two excellent alternatives nearby, however, with cafés, deckchairs, and snorkeling gear for rent.

At the fork, another path (a steep 350m/380yds) heads left to **Blue Lagoon**, an adorable beach that almost disappears at high tide. The other is **Bias Tugel**, about 800m (900yds) up from the other end of the village, past the morning market and in front of the skeletal remains of another unfinished resort. **Snorkeling** to other places, such as Tanjung Jepun, can be arranged with boatmen (who also rent gear) at stalls along the main (beach) street. More serious underwater exploration is available from **scuba diving** agencies, notably Absolute Scuba (absolutescubabali.com) and Geko Dive (gekodive.com). Topi Inn (topiinn.net) offers **workshops** in music, dance, and cooking, as well as guides for **hiking**.

Getting There Padangbai is 2km (1.2 miles) from the main road between Denpasar and Amlapura. Shuttle buses connect with the main tourist centers, and *bemo* go to/from Semarapura and Amlapura.
Tip There are numerous places to stay, though most restaurants offer better views than the hotels
Also nearby Tenganan and Semarapura

5 Ulu Watu Temple, South Bali
A stunning cliff-top setting with Bali's best *Kecak* dance

Perched on a rocky outcrop along the southwest tip of Bukit Peninsula, **Pura Luhur Ulu Watu** temple is certainly less touristy than its sister at Tanah Lot, but also less impressive. The grounds aren't nearly as extensive and the temple itself is underwhelming: small, newly-renovated, and closed to non-Hindus. But Ulu Watu is understandably popular for the cliff-top setting 80m (260ft) above the crashing waves and even more so for the extraordinary *Kecak* dance. The low-key atmosphere with zero souvenir stalls and hawkers is also definitely part of the charm. Constructed about 1,000 years ago (but rebuilt many times since) and dedicated to the gods of the sea, Ulu Watu is one of Bali's six revered cardinal temples. It's renowned for the arched gateway guarded by monuments of Ganesha, the sacred elephant-headed god, and particularly crowded and photogenic during the **Galungan festival** (see page 117). Ulu Watu is also home to hundreds of kleptomaniacal monkeys, so hang on to your hats, sunglasses, and handbags! But the main reason why the car park is overflowing from 5pm is the *Kecak* dance held in a special amphitheater at sunset (6-7pm). This show with its spectacular lights and music is more dramatic and entertaining than the one at Tanah Lot. (Tickets go on sale at 5pm at an unsigned counter near the temple entrance.) Unlike Tanah Lot, however, there's nowhere to **eat** or **drink** inside the Ulu Watu complex, and the cliff-side **paths** peter out quickly, but they do offer the best photos of the three-tiered pagoda and the thunderous surf pounding the cliffs below.

Times Daily 8am–7pm **Address** Signposted from Pecatu in central Bukit Peninsula **Dress** Entrance fee includes a sarong and sash **Getting There** On organized tours; there's no public transport or waiting taxis. **Tips** A few eateries around the car park offer basic Indonesian fare. The best time for views, photos, and serenity is before 10am. There are several nearby homestays along the road to Ulu Watu beach. **Also nearby** Jimbaran, Garuda Wisnu Kencana Cultural Park, and Ulu Watu beach

6 Pasir Putih Beach, East Bali
One of Bali's best beaches remains blissfully undeveloped

Only 6km (4 miles) northeast of Candidasa in Perasi village a small sign indicates a turn-off to "White Sands Beach," the unimaginative name (translated into English) given to one of Bali's very best. The calm waters are perfect for **swimming** and **snorkeling**—with no surf (or surfer dudes)—and the sand is white, a rarity along this stretch of the coast. It's also an ideal place to lay down your towel and splash about if you're staying at Candidasa, which is a beach resort without an actual beach. Pasir Putih is long and curved, flanked by cliffs offering shade and snorkeling, and backed by fields of coconut palms where kids playing soccer share the grass with cattle. The far end of the beach is lined with *jukung* fishing boats and huts where women weave nets and men build boats. Pasir Putih is a simple fishing village. There's nowhere to stay (and hopefully never will be), but beachside **food stalls** do offer the freshest grilled fish possible and cold

drinks, such as *kelapa muda* (young coconut) in its shell. You can rent deckchairs and **snorkeling equipment** and arrange a **massage**, so you could spend all day here—and come back again the next and the next… Another attraction is the gorgeous scenery along the 1.6km (1 mile) flat, shady, and deserted road from the sign in Perasi. Along the way, you'll pass friendly locals collecting firewood, buffaloes ploughing rice fields, and paths leading into wild coconut groves. The road finishes at a small car park with a temple and entry post, where we beg, beseech, and implore you to leave any vehicle. From there, the 500m (540yd) path to the beach is very rough, so please walk there instead. The village is not a car park. Better still, park in, and walk from, Perasi.

Getting There *Bemo* to Amlapura from Semarapura or Padangbai to the turn-off in Perasi; from there, walk or there may be an *ojek* (motorbike taxi) **Also nearby** Tenganan and Ujung water palace

7 Tirtagangga Water Palace
Fountains and lotus ponds surrounded by rice fields

The **Taman Tirtagangga** complex was built over 60 years ago by the final regional king who was clearly obsessed with water palaces and based this one on the Palace of Versailles in France; well, sort of. Named after the Ganges River in India, the palace was destroyed, like many other buildings in eastern Bali, during the eruption of Gunung Agung in 1963, but the gardens (not the palace) have been lovingly rebuilt. With fountains, statues and stepping stones across ponds choked with lotus flowers, Tirtagangga is much more of a **garden** than a collection of buildings, and more appealing than the other water palaces at Ujung and Semarapura. Tirtagangga is tranquil, superbly-maintained and often refreshingly empty, because tour groups just dash in and out during the middle of the day. The two spring-fed **pools** look inviting, but the water is quite cold and there's no privacy, and the changing sheds are decrepit. The countryside,

especially behind the Good Karma restaurant at the car park, is begging to be explored on foot but, of course, trails are designed for locals traversing between rice fields and villages and not for **hiking**. (See Best Walks on page 114 for more details.) Tirtagangga is somewhere to linger, not rush; a place to soak up the fresh, cool air and admire the **views** of Agung and, sometimes, Rinjani volcano on Lombok. Better still, stay at a homestay nearby or at the magnificent **Tirtu Ayu Hotel** (see Best Hotels on page 78) inside the gardens. At least, stay for lunch and/or the stupendous **sunset**.

Times Daily 8am–6pm **Dress** A sign asks visitors to "dress appropriately." If swimming, please dress modestly: not in Kuta-kini swimwear. **Getting There** Along the road between Amlapura and Culik. Go on an organized tour; take a *bemo* between Amlapura and Abang or Culik; or by Perama shuttle bus from Padangbai or Candidasa (minimum of two) **Also nearby** Tenganan, and the east coast road between Ujung and Amed

8 Cycling on Nusa Lembongan Island
Discover what Bali must've been like fifty years ago

Although located between the southern beaches of Bali and Gili Trawangan, Nusa Lembongan is like neither: there are no mini-marts or nightclubs; not even a post office. And there are no cars, so with the perfect combination of (mostly) paved and flat roads, and zero traffic, it's ideal for cycling—although a mountain bike and heavy-duty leg muscles are needed for the hilly interior. Start your trip from **Jungutbatu**, where bikes can be rented from shops and guesthouses. A flat road (1.2km/0.75 miles) passes through Jungutbatu village and beach before becoming progressively pot-holed as it leads (2.2km/1.3 miles) to **Mangrove Beach**. Along the way you'll pass **seaweed farms** and often need to stop to "ooh" and "aah" at the jaw-dropping double-layered views of the volcanoes on the Bali mainland. Mangrove Beach is a dead end, so go back (1.4km/0.86 miles) to the obvious and only turn-off and follow the flat road (4.8km/3 miles) south through the uninhabitable **mangrove forest**—which is even more eerie at high tide—as far as the next

T-junction. You now have three options: (1) pedal across the island to Jungutbatu (1.8km/1.1 miles) along a road that's steepish in both directions, but doable; (2) head back (4.2km/2.6 miles) to the shortcut (at the new *bale* meeting hall) which leads back to the road that passes Jungutbatu beach; or (3) continue for a hilly, but not too steep, 3.4km (2.1 miles) to **Lembongan village**. If you choose option three, you can then detour across the rickety suspension bridge to **Nusa Ceningan** and stop for sweeping **views** of the remarkable harbor clogged with seaweed farms. From the T-junction in Lembongan village, it's a flat 1.2km (0.75 miles) to Dream, Sunset, or Mushroom **beaches**. Otherwise, complete the Lembongan loop back to Jungutbatu along a road that is Tour-de France-steep heading in the other direction, but surprisingly manageable going north.

Getting There Refer to page 62 for details about boats to/from Bali **Tip** To avoid the steep bits, stick to the road between Jungutbatu and Mangrove Beach, and the one through the mangrove forest along the east coast.

9 Ubud's Taman Saraswati Dances
Bali's best dance performances are in a temple in Ubud

One of the "toughest" decisions you'll have to make is which of the multitude of traditional dances to attend—and where. A leaflet from the tourist office in Ubud lists 13 types of performances held at 18 different locations. (Refer to Best Dance Performances on pages 110–11 for more information about what to see.) But unless you're an aficionado of Balinese dance and music, you'll probably be more interested in the *where* than the *which*, and no setting in Ubud, and probably the rest of Bali, is more delightful for a traditional performance than **Pura Taman Saraswati**. The temple's location is not only elegant but also convenient, and the audience can sit comfortably close to the stage with the pond behind and the temple as a backdrop. Built 60 years ago and dedicated to the Goddess of the Arts, the temple is renowned for the pond choked with lotus flowers, so it's often called the "Lotus Pond Open Stage." The gardens and pond can be visited during the day but only Hindus are allowed inside the temple. Otherwise, you can admire the whole complex, and enjoy the serenity only meters from the comparative chaos outside, at the attached Café Lotus or the amazingly congruous Starbucks. (Diners at Café Lotus can watch a traditional dance from the restaurant, but only patrons in the front row will be charged for a ticket.) Taman Saraswati hosts a *Janger* Dance (Sunday); Women's *Gamelan* & Children's Dance (Tuesday); *Barong* & Children's Dance (Thursday); and a bright, enthusiastic combination including a *Legong* dance on Saturday.

Times One hour (7.30–8.30pm) **Cost** Rp80,000 (fixed price); no reserved seating **Address** Jalan Raya Ubud **Dress** As you wish **Tip** Patrons in the first few rows may be invited to join a dance at the end! **Add in** Dinner at Café Lotus or an après-show drink at the Jazz Café Tebesaya

10 Rice Terraces at Jatiluwih
An indescribable amphitheater of cascading rice fields

Words cannot describe the sheer beauty of the rice field terraces at Jatiluwih, where emerald-green amphitheaters cascade down the slopes under the omnipotent glare of four volcanoes, including Bali's second highest, Gunung Batukau (2,271m/7,450ft). You'll be stopping every 3.6 seconds to take photos, marvel at the skills required to tend and harvest the *padi* fields, and wonder how they were even chiseled from the rocky landscape centuries ago. It's so extraordinary that UNESCO has recognized the area for its beauty and the ancient methods of growing, harvesting and irrigating the rice. Much of it is *padi Bali*, a taller and more nutritious variety of rice that only grows once a year. The area is now a popular stopover for the rash of eco-buggy-nature-cycling-adventure-trekking companies that have blossomed unabated in recent years. But the rice fields are not designed for **hiking**, although opposite the Warung Teras Subak café a walking **trail** has been created along a ridge providing astonishing 360-degree **views**. The road that weaves alongside the rice fields is about 4km (2.5 miles) long, starting from Warung Jatiluwih, the first of the **buffet restaurants**, to the last, Billy's Terrace Café, which also offers the best views. Few venture onwards along the atrocious road to **Pura Luhur Batukau**, one of Bali's most revered temples high on the slopes of Batukau (see page 54). Inevitably, there are plenty of places to stop, **eat,** and admire the views, as well as a few **homestays**.

Address There's a turn-off at Baturiti, along the road between Denpasar and Candikuning/Bedugul, but it's probably more convenient from the road starting at the "Corn Cob Statue" in Candikuning. Always follow signs to "Senganan" and "Jatiluwih 259" (the name of the road). **Getting There** There's no public transport, but it is included on some organized tours. Otherwise, charter an *ojek* (motorbike taxi) from Candikuning. **Tip** Bring a jumper and wet weather gear in case **Also nearby** Bedugul, and the temple at Lake Bratan

11 Ubud's Monkey Forest
Eerie temples, forest walks, and cheeky primates

This area of lush forest, more formally known as Mandala Wisata Wanara Wana, is perched at the bottom end of a busy shopping street. It's home to hundreds of cute but recalcitrant Balinese Macaques, which are tolerated, and even revered, as descendants of the monkey god Hanoman who saved the wife of King Rama (as told in the *Ramayana* epic). But beware: they can be menacing if they think you're carrying anything curved or yellow. Tickets to the sanctuary include a useful map with locations and explanations of the three temples, each originally built in the 14th century. They are not, however, accessible to non-Hindus, but small enough to admire from the outside. One path leads up to **Pura Prajapati** temple, used for cremations and burials by the Padangtegal village nearby, and flanked by a leafy field of headstones. Another path heads to **Pura Dalem Agung Padangtegal**, the "death temple" used by the same villagers for ceremonies. And a third walkway goes over a medieval-looking stone bridge — seemingly held together by roots of banyan trees like a scene from *The Lord of the Rings* movie — to the **Holy Bathing Temple**. Also worth a look is the **Community Art Exhibition** under the *bale* pavilion, and check at the ticket offices about events and performances at the brand new **amphitheater**. Noteworthy for being well managed by the local community, the forest is also home to 115 species of rare plants used for religious and medicinal purposes. The main entrance is at the end of the road named after the sanctuary. Another

gate, 200m (218yds) further east, is connected by a path (800m/874yds) to a third entrance that leads to the charming village of **Nyuhkuning**.

Times Daily 8.30am–6pm **Address** Monkey Forest Road (Jalan Wanara Wana) **Dress** As you wish; no sarong/sash needed **Getting There** By foot from Ubud; on organized tours from elsewhere **Tip** Quieter with less hyper-active monkeys before 10am **Add in** Shopping along Jalan Hanoman and lunch in Nyuhkuning

12 Gunung Kawi Rock Temples

Majestic shrines chiselled into a solid stone cliff face

Gunung Kawi has it all: massive rock sculptures, gushing streams, lush rice-terraces, caves dripping with water, and a riverside temple. And steep steps. Lots of them. More than 250, in fact. If you don't make it all the way down, only 40 or 50 steps will lead you to exquisite **views** of *padi* fields flanking the Pakrisan River under the shadow of the mighty Gunung Agung mountain. The steps do eventually end at **The Royal Monuments**, four massive façades shaped like temples and somehow carved into 7-meter (23-ft) high niches within a cliff. They may have been built as a memorial for King Airlangga, a powerful Javanese king, some 1,000 years ago, but no one really knows for sure. Across a quaint bridge, **Pura Tirta Gunung Kawi** temple is dedicated to the all-important Goddess of Rice. At the back of the pond crammed with fish are five more **royal tombs** built directly opposite the ravine from the other four. Walking **paths**

behind the temple lead to storage and cooking sheds, and then continue to a **shrine** facing a mossy cliff, a series of watery **caves** (once part of a monastery) and the best **views** of the whole complex. But before you explore the area too much further: remember all those steps on the way back! Then you can reward yourself at **Kafe Kawi**, a delightful restaurant only 10 steps down from the main entrance, which offers a varied menu, including healthy breakfasts (from 9am) and, of course, more superb views.

Time Daily 7am–6pm **Address** 200m (218yds) from the main road through Tampaksiring **Dress** As you wish; sash/sarong included in entrance fee **Getting There** On many organized tours. From Ubud, *bemo* towards Gianyar, get off at the junction in Bedulu, then catch another to Tampaksiring. *Ojek* available at the site. **Tips** Better photos and fewer people before 9am. This shouldn't be confused with Gunung Kawi in nearby Sebatu, which is also worth visiting (see page 46). **Also nearby** Walk up to Tirta Empul, or visit the other Gunung Kawi at Sebatu

13 Banjar Village, North Bali
Hot springs and Bali's only Buddhist monastery

Nestled in the foothills near Lovina, Banjar has a plethora of **temples** and a busy produce **market** that spreads across the main street each morning. But the village is more renowned for its well-maintained **hot springs** located in a lush, tropical setting. Visitors can splash about in the hot-water pools or stand under dragon-shaped spouts for a massaging spray. The complex is agreeably set up with lockers, showers, and massage rooms, but come early or late because the hot sun and hot water do not mix well, and there's no pool with cold water. And avoid weekends and public holidays, although these are great times to watch locals enjoy themselves (which can be half the fun sometimes). Banjar is also home to **Brahmavihara Arama** (0362-92954), Bali's only Buddhist **monastery**. Although not as impressive as those found in Thailand, it does offer the sort of serene location, extensive gardens, and **coastal views** that you'd find in a five star resort. Under the stupas, reminiscent of a miniature version of the Borobudur temple in Java, Buddhists are welcome to meditate, while others may contemplate in huts perched along the lower slopes. While tourists are welcome,

this is a functioning monastery (though oddly devoid of monks) and not a designated tourist attraction, nor a retreat for foreigners. This may change, however, with the imminent construction inside of… yes, bungalows. Both attractions can be visited separately or together by **walking**, which is described further in Best Walks (see page 114).

Times Springs (8am–6pm daily); monastery (dawn to dusk daily) **Dress** Modest swimwear (springs); borrow a sarong there if you're wearing shorts/skirt (monastery) **Getting There** Turn-offs to both are accessible by *bemo* from Lovina and then *ojek*. To the springs, follow signs to *air panas* ("hot water"). To the monastery, follow the road to Pedawa. The turn-off between the springs and monastery is at the market. **Tip** A homestay and *warung* at the springs **Also nearby** Sing Sing Waterfalls and Lovina

14 Mount Batur Natural Hot Springs
Hot and cold volcanic pools by a spectacular crater lake

The largest lake in Bali is nestled inside the island's most active volcano. Most stop along the crater rim of **Gunung Batur** to photo the lava-coated slopes, pig out at the buffet table and curse a hawker, but few realize there's much more to enjoy inside the volcano. The road from Penelokan leads to the main lakeside village of Toya Bungkah, where three places offer pools of spring-fed hot water and contrasting cold. Each shares the same sources of water, features similarly magnificent views and provides massages (for an extra payment), but facilities differ markedly. And, despite claims, none provide spas with any "healing powers." The **public baths** (also known as *Tamba*) are squeezed between the two resorts. While more palatable after recent renovations, the pools are small, not private, and smell of sulphur. There's also nowhere to sit and relax, but it is the cheapest option (Rp50,000). Next door, **Batur Natural Hot Spring** (0366-

51193; baturhotspring.com) charges Rp120,000 (including towel, snack, drink, shower, and locker); Rp160,000 including lunch. The uninviting car park belies an attractive, spacious setting, but there are few places to lounge about and it caters mainly for Indonesians, so you may be the only foreigner there. Visiting the lakeside **restaurant** doesn't require a ticket, however, and **bicycles** can be rented. **Toya Devasya** (0366-51204; toyadevasya.com) is a luxurious Seminyak-style resort with a massive cold-water swimming pool and two hot-water baths. It's excellent value at Rp150,000 (including towel, drink, shower, and locker), and with a pool-bar and plethora of lounge chairs it un-ashamedly caters for spoilt westerners. Onsite there are also some pricey **villas** and a lakeside **restaurant** called The Lakeside Restaurant.

Times All three open 7am–7pm daily **Getting There** To crater rim, *bemo* from Gianyar, Semarapura, or Singaraja, or Perama shuttle bus (minimum of two) from Kuta, Sanur, or Ubud; then *ojek* to Toya Bungkah and the springs **Tip** There are several places to stay and eat in Toya Bungkah, but places in Kedisan are further from the incessant truck traffic.

15 From Ujung to Amed, East Bali
Weave around the coast through tiny fishing villages

The driest part of Bali is not the most scenic, but the landscapes and **views** are quite unique. And now that the road hugging the far eastern coast has been fully paved, the trip is far more enjoyable. The road is still windy and narrow, however, and there's no public transport, but you will be rewarded with some of the island's best panoramas, and villages where adults smile and children wave at the rare sight of a white face. From Padangbai, avoid Amlapura and its infuriating one-way streets by turning right at the junction to Pantai Jasri and then almost immediately turn left towards the Amlapura-Ujung road. After exploring the water palace at **Ujung**, follow the road markers to "sry" (Seraya) and then "clk" (Culik). The picturesque route is dotted with villagers eking out a subsistence living from fishing, logging, and selling the sort of rocks that line paths in the resorts down south. The road heads inland to **Seraya** where an idyllic hilltop **temple** offers **views** of the village and

coastline. Soon you'll be winding your way along scarred, terraced **mountain slopes** where attempts have been made, with limited success, to plant trees and grow vegetables in the harsh, arid landscape. Then the **fishing villages** appear. The most dramatic spot to photograph these is near the "clk 17" marker, where an abandoned lookout is perched on a rocky promontory. From "clk 13," a series of villages—known collectively as **Amed**—starts, but the **beaches** are disappointing: always gray, mostly rocky and often lined with fishing vessels. The road then heads inland with more oh-my-god-stop-the-car! **views**—this time of Mount Agung. At the dreary T-junction hub of Culik, the road continues to Singaraja, via Tulamben, or veers left past sudden valleys of lush rice fields towards Tirtagangga.

Getting There Shuttle bus (minimum of two) from Lovina or Padangbai to northern Amed, via Culik—not via Ujung **Tip** Time your trip for a seafood lunch along Amed **Also nearby** Tirtagangga water palace

16 Snorkeling Lombok's Gili Islands
Some of the world's best diving right under your nose

Imagine three droplets of golden sands surrounded by turquoise seas where the only form of transport is bicycle and *cidomo* (horse and cart). But for many, the major attractions are underwater: 3,500 species of **marine life**—double the number found at Australia's Great Barrier Reef—including coral fish of every imaginable hue, as well as harmless sharks and giant (protected) turtles. Although some reefs have been partially destroyed by boats and fish-bombing, some of the coral and marine life is even accessible from the beach, so snorkelers can explore the sort of underwater delights normally only available to those with tanks. Masks, snorkels and fins are cheap and easy to rent and stall-owners should be able to point you to the best locations. Otherwise, an understandably popular alternative is a trip on a glass bottomed boat (only Rp120,000 per person, including lunch and snorkeling gear) which takes you to the best spots around all three islands to see and swim among turtles, clams, fish, and coral. There are also many wonderful places for do-it-yourself snorkeling just offshore. On Gili Trawangan, try in front of the Bale Sampan hotel (north-east coast) and at Turtle Point (north)—but don't venture too far because currents can be deceptively strong. Very close to Gili Air's appealing beaches, snorkeling is excellent near the Blue Marlin Dive center (north-east coast), Hotel Gili Air (north) and, especially, Air Wall (west). The best spots from the beaches of Gili Meno are Meno Wall (north-west coast), which abounds with turtles, while amazing marine life can be observed opposite the Royal Reef Resort (east), Ana Bungalows (north), and the abandoned Bounty Resort (south-west).

Getting There Refer to page 62 for details about boats to/from Bali **Tip** The range and cost of scuba diving and boat trips is best on Gili Trawangan.

17 Southern Lombok's Kuta Beach
Solitude that is oh so different from Bali's Kuta

ombok's Kuta (sometimes written
Kute) could not contrast more to its
(in)famous namesake on Bali: imagine a
place where tourists are outnumbered in
the sea by fishermen and on the beach by
goats; and as surfers spread east and west
during the day searching for those gnarly
waves, stallholders in bamboo huts gossip
while waiting for customers to saunter
past. A few stalls offer **surfing** lessons,
board rentals and repairs, as well as **boat
trips**—but these are really token offers by
boat-owners and of minimal interest to
visitors (and getting the minimum required to make it cost-effective may be
difficult). The beach is perfect for swimming—sheltered, shallow and surfer-
free—although the eastern end at the
village is scruffy. (Refer to page 69 for
information about **swimming** and **snorkeling** further along the southern coast.)
Other activities include **horse riding**
along deserted beaches with Kuta Horses
(0819-15999436) and **bicycle tours**
organized by the Solah restaurant (so-
lahlombok.com). The major **scuba diving**
agency—Scuba Froggy (scubafroggy.
com)—offers a range of dive trips as far
east as Ekas and west as Gili Nanggu. Oh,
and two other things: Kuta is home to the

remarkable **Bau Nyale** festival (see page
118) and one of the best weekly **markets**
(Sunday morning) you'll see anywhere. This
Kuta remains an anachronism reminiscent
of its boisterous namesake from the 1970s.
Tourist facilities remain basic, resorts virtually non-existent, and transport options
limited, but this will surely change soon as
the international airport has relocated nearby. The latest news is that the same company (BTDC) that built and runs Nusa Dua
wants to create the Mandalika Tourism
Precinct along 7.5km (4.6 miles) of Kuta's
finest beaches with a golf course, theme
park and—*gulp*—motor-racing track.

Getting There *Bemo* connections to Praya are
infrequent, so take a "shuttle bus" (often just a
shared car) to major tourist destinations on
Lombok and further afield to Bali and Sumbawa.

18 Lombok's Senaru Village

A quaint village on the slopes of a towering volcano

Clinging to the northern slopes of the mighty Rinjani volcano, Senaru is known as the best place to start and/or finish a trek to the summit or crater lake, but the village is certainly worth visiting for other reasons. The **views** of Mt. Rinjani and the northern coastline are splendid from anywhere along the 4km-long ridge upon which Senaru and the adjoining village of Batu Koq are nestled. And the gentle **walks** through lush forests to the thunderous **waterfalls** are so good they deserve their own section (see Best Walks on page 115). At the point where the road ends and the trail starts is the **Rinjani Trek Center**, which offers some informative but faded posters along its walls about the **Gunung Rinjani National Park**. Opposite, **Kampung Tradisional Senaru**, a "traditional village" with a few thatched huts, is probably less wor-

thy of your time. About 45 minutes' stroll downhill—and accessible on the way back by *bemo* if you're lucky, or *ojek* (motorbike taxi)—is **Bayan**, center for the Islamic sect of Wektu Telu with its unique thatched **mosques**. The trailhead can be congested for a few minutes every day, but most trekkers these days buzz in and out of Senaru with immediate connections to Senggigi or the Gili Islands, so the village remains delightfully **tranquil**. Other reasons to visit and stay a while are easy access from Senggigi and the Gilis; fresher air and cooler **weather** than anywhere along the sticky coastline; rustic **homestays** (read: no resorts) with million-dollar views of rice-terraced valleys and waterfalls; and the chance to try traditional **Sasak food** at simple *warung* food stalls (read: no western-style restaurants).

Getting There *Bemo* from Sweta (Mandalika) terminal in Mataram to Bayan, then *ojek* to Senaru. Easy to charter or share a "shuttle bus" (normally just a car) from Senggigi. **Tip** Stay in or near Pondok Senaru in the village "center" because the main road is steep.

19 Pura Lingsar Temple in Lombok
Sacred to Hindus and Muslims who "fight" with rice cakes

Not far from the capital, Mataram, and easily accessible from Senggigi, **Pura Lingsar** is the most important and sacred temple on Lombok. Built in the 18th century by a Balinese ruler and based on various animist beliefs, the temple is now revered by Hindus as well as followers of a minority sect of unorthodox Islam known as Wektu Telu (although followers are officially referred to as Muslims). But worshippers of Buddhism, Christianity, and orthodox Islam also come to pray, make offerings for a good harvest and bountiful rain, and to bathe in the holy waters. The more elevated **Pura Gaduh** Hindu temple has four shrines pointing towards the twin volcanic powers of Rinjani (Lombok) and Agung (Bali). The lower Wektu Telu **Kemaliq** building has two courtyards with Balinese-style architecture—one for praying, the other with a pond. Gates to the pond are opened if someone buys hard-boiled eggs at the entrance and a priest or guardian can be found to lure eels to the surface of the pond. (Observing the eels is regarded by locals as a sign of good fortune.) The setting is also delightful, with immaculate **gardens**, **walking** paths heading in all directions to *padi* fields and a large pool. (But be wary of stumbling into segregated

and unsigned public bathing areas.) The temple is especially popular on Sundays and public holidays, and at its most colorful during **Perang Topat** ("Rice Cake War"). Part of the Pujawali festival in late November or early December, this is when Hindus and Muslims engage in good-natured rivalry by throwing food, mostly rice cakes called *topat*, at each other. Tourists are not immune from being targets and everyone is encouraged to participate.

Times Daylight hours daily **Dress** Rent sarong/sash at temple entrance **Getting There** *Bemo* from Sweta (Mandalika) terminal in Mataram to Lingsar village. **Tips** A donation of Rp5,000 is enough. A guide is not compulsory, despite what you may be told. **Also nearby** Taman Narmada park

20 Lombok's Senggigi Beach
A resort with deserted beaches and quiet roads. No, really!

Stretching north from the island's capital Mataram is a series of glorious, curved beaches interrupted by rocky promontories and backed by undeveloped hills covered with dense coconut groves. A popular spot for tourists to photograph the **views** (especially at sunset)—and for the sizable local Balinese population to pray—is the picturesque Hindu temple, **Pura Batu Bolong**, which faces the mighty Agung volcano on Bali. While supremely photogenic, the **beaches** are a mixed bag for **swimming**, and most sand is grayish. The two best beaches in Central Senggigi are in front of the Aerowisata and Sheraton hotels, but the public beach in between both is scruffy and impossibly busy on weekends. More alluring are the beaches at **Mangsit**, a few kilometers north, and between Café Alberto and Pura Batu Bolong temple, while you can almost feel Crusoe-esque along stretches of sand south of the temple. At breakwaters in front of the Aerowisata hotel, fishermen compete for

the waves with local (not foreign) **surfers**; this is also the best area for **snorkeling** (and the only place to rent equipment anyway). Ignored by almost every foreign tourist, and only 1.2km (0.75 miles) from the main road, is the **Taman Wisata Alam Kerandangan nature reserve**, a dense sanctuary of hiking trails, waterfalls and, of course, monkeys. For many, the appeal of Senggigi is what it *doesn't* have: tourist hordes, heavy traffic, and high prices. It's more spacious and tranquil than the Kuta/Legian region of Bali, but also smaller and less developed. In addition, Senggigi is a perfect base for **exploring western Lombok**, but be warned: many hotel rooms in central Senggigi are within earshot of at least one (and often three) nightclubs.

Getting There *Bemo* (i.e., pick-up trucks) ply the main road as far as Kebun Roek terminal in Ampenan (western Mataram). Shuttle buses depart for all major tourist spots in Bali and Lombok. **Tip** Don't stay in central Senggigi unless you're a heavy clubber or heavier sleeper.

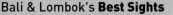

21 Taman Narmada Gardens, Lombok
The closest you may get to Rinjani and its crater lake

Once upon a time, there was a bored king who lived in eastern Bali but ruled this part of Lombok, and had an obsession with Gunung Rinjani... King Anak Agung Ngurah Gede Karang Asem built what was probably used as a summer palace in 1727. It was designed to pay homage to the might of Lombok's only volcano, the omnipotent Rinjani, which he could see but no longer climb for his annual pilgrimage. (Although it is just possible the King may have also enjoyed watching young girls bathe in the pools.) The park features the **Pura Kalasa** temple, described on the billboard at the entrance as a "mini Rinjani"—which is a slight exaggeration considering the original is 3,726m (12,224ft) high. To complete the "Rinjani replica," the **Asem Pool** is shaped (sort of) like the Danau Segara Anak crater lake that sits on top of Rinjani. But, perhaps, the King would be most displeased that the pool is now used by canoodling couples in paddle

boats. Taman Narmada is such an attractive place to wander around and admire the fountains, ponds and flowers, to **swim** in the pools, to relax under large shady trees and to appreciate the architecture featuring Sasak, Javanese, Islamic, and Balinese designs. And you can shop for **souvenirs** in the stalls on the way out. Like most places in this region, you may have the place to yourself during the week, but half of Mataram seems to flock here on weekends and public holidays, and anyone with a white face (if you have one) may become the center of attraction. The **market** at the *bemo* stop at the entrance sells a more noteworthy selection of **handicrafts** than usual.

Times 7am–6pm daily **Getting There** *Bemo* from Senggigi to Kebun Roek terminal in Ampenan in Mataram; then another to the Narmada market directly opposite the park entrance. Otherwise, charter a car or taxi. **Also nearby** Pura Lingsar temple

CHAPTER 2
EXPLORING BALI & LOMBOK

Almost every conceivable type of attraction and activity is available on Bali and Lombok. But perhaps you're only interested in shopping, surfing, and partying, or you just want to relax away from the crowds along Bali's northern or eastern coasts or on Lombok. Possibly, you're yearning to explore the villages and temples of Bali's spiritual heartland from Ubud, or maybe climbing volcanoes, rafting rivers, and snorkeling reefs are your thing. Whatever your interests, this chapter provides detailed daily excursions (and some vital extra special sections) that includes all the information you need to know about where to go, how to get there, and what to see.

1 Southern Bali
2 Ubud
3 Bali's East Coast
4 Bali's Highlands & North Coast
5 The Nusa Islands
6 Western Lombok
7 Northern Lombok
8 Southern Lombok

EXPLORING SOUTHERN BALI
This epicenter for tourism has more to offer than many realize

Also see Sanur and Nusa Dua & Tanjung Benoa insets on the folded map

Sometime in the 1970s, the Bali Big Bang occurred and a malarial fishing village called Kuta quickly turned into one of the most popular tourist destinations on earth. Maybe 70 percent of visitors to Bali stay in, and rarely venture from, the southern beaches. Although this region continues to expand unabated, among the malls and resorts, homestays and tattoo parlors, there is village life where temples abound and markets flourish.

Day 1: Kuta Beach
Bali's fabled tourist Mecca

B egin your exploration on foot after breakfast, but if shopping is your primary interest there's no point starting until the stores open at 9am. But remember: walking around Kuta/Legian is rarely pleasant and never easy: pram-pushers will find it impossible, and dual-tasking

walker/texters have been known to disappear down drain holes. Take your time, and don't forget that taxis are very common and cheap.

The best place to start walking is the center of the original **Kuta**, where Jalan Legian starts at the corner with Jalan Pantai Kuta. This intersection is still known as "*bemo* corner," although this form of public transport disappeared from Kuta years ago. About 200m (218yds) east, a traditional produce **market** is set up every morning, but understandably dissipates before the traffic starts snarling at 8am. Continuing along Jalan Pantai Kuta towards the beach, **Kuta Square** is dominated by the old-fashioned **Matahari department store**, but is outclassed these days by the massive **Discovery Shopping Center** 800m (874yds) south along Jalan Dewi Sartika in Tuban. Easy to spot just south of the Matahari, the **Kuta Art Market** is a misnomer as most stalls sell nothing but T-shirts, sunglasses, and watches—unless phallic-shaped bottle-openers count as "art." The adjacent **Pura Dalem Pakendungan** temple proves that some normality can still prevail amongst the Kuta chaos.

Further south, parts of **Tuban** are reminiscent of a fishing village and worth detouring along the delightful, shady path as far as the airport fence (see Best Walks on page 112). The beaches are a bit

Relaxing on Kuta beach

scruffy, especially where hotels have no vested interest, but noteworthy because they're set up for the Balinese and Indonesian tourists, not foreigners. If you head south along the path through Tuban for about 1km (0.62 miles), you will come across **Pura Dalem Tunon**, the most elegant beachside temple between Tanah Lot and Ulu Watu. In contrast is **Waterbom Park**, an immense assortment of pools, slides, and rides more popular, it seems, with adults than kids (see page 93). It's along Jalan Dewi Sartika, 350m (382yds) south of the art market.

Only meters south from where Jalan Pantai Kuta meets the beach is the **Sea Turtle Information Center**, obvious from the giant statue of a *penyu* outside. It offers a limited display about their laudable efforts to conserve these graceful creatures. Continuing north along the beach road is **Pura Batu Bolong** temple, incongruously located between the familiar "golden arches" and the massive new **Beachwalk** shopping and entertainment complex, which is particularly popular with kids (see page 93).

For some, Kuta is also synonymous with tragedy. One year, one month, and one day after the attacks on the World Trade Center in 2001, terrorists struck Paddy's Bar and the Sari Club. The poignant **Bali Memorial**, positioned at what is dubbed "ground zero," lists the names and nationalities of the dead, which included 88 Australians and 38 Indonesians. A cathartic attraction for many, particularly young Australians, it's situated where Poppies Lane II (Jalan Batu Bolong) meets the main road (Jalan Legian).

And Jalan Legian is anarchic: vehicles barely move as they struggle through the bewildering one- and two-way traffic system, while tourists walking faster battle persistent hawkers, potholed footpaths, and construction sites. But somehow along Jalan Benesari, the next main street that heads back to the beach, coconut groves and original surfer homestays have survived the decades of developmental onslaught.

Soon you'll be in **Legian**, a subtle mix of Kuta's crassness and Seminyak's sophistication. Continue along the pleasant beachside **walkway** (mostly devoid of vehicles, so popular with **cyclists**), which is lined with charming two-story **restaurants**, ideal for sunset watching. Stroll further up the beach, or detour back up Jalan Legian where things become dearer and trendier as the road changes to Jalan Raya Seminyak—shops are called boutiques and restaurants turn into bistros, and there are chic galleries like **Biasa Artspace** (see page 100).

What is often lumped together in maps and books as "Seminyak" are really two different places: Seminyak and Petitenget. Seminyak was a haven for expatriates until they started moving north to Petitenget as tourists headed up from Kuta. It's probably now time for lunch, so try one of the enticing on-beach cafes such as La Plancha or The Champlung, both a reverent distance from the black-rock **Pura Dalem Camplung** temple. These two eateries are particularly alluring from late in the afternoon when bean bags are sprawled across the sand so you can savor the sunset and enjoy live music after dark.

Turn right just up along the beachside path at Jalan Abimanyu. Tucked away among construction sites is the elegant Protestant **St Mikael's Church**. Immaculately white and surrounded by lush gardens, it's open for Sunday services and worth a look at other times. Continue walking along the sand (the promenade unfortunately stops) or up Jalan Sari Dewi. This quiet road and the area north of Jalan

Laksmana are ideal for **cycling**, but surprisingly the only place that rents bicycles is the SP Midi supermarket (Jalan Camplung Tanduk, Seminyak).

Soon you'll be in shopping heaven at Jalan Laksmana (see page 86), which leads to **Petitenget** (which means "magic box"). Finish your exploration at the 16th century **Pura Petitenget** temple (also signposted as "Pura Masceti"), which you can visit provided your knees and arms are suitably covered (no sarongs can be borrowed/rented).

If you have any time and energy left after all that walking, shopping, and eating, take a taxi to **Tanah Lot**, one of the most revered temples in Bali (and described in detail on page 9). Starting by mid-afternoon, you can avoid the hordes flocking there later for the sunset, and detour to beaches around **Canggu**, where future developmental onslaught is probably inevitable. Although these beaches are scruffy, with less appealing gray volcanic sand and minimal facilities, these side trips offer serene countryside of duck-filled *padi* fields. The nicest stretch of road leads to **Pantai Seseh** beach.

In contrast, the entrance to Tanah Lot is overrun with an extraordinary array of souvenir stalls. Allow time to wander along the cliff-top paths that offer superb views of the temple and of the waves crashing against the rocks below. Then, choose a front row seat at one of the cafés opposite the temple and enjoy a drink during the much-photographed sunset.

Unfortunately, thousands of others will also be sharing your experience. You can avoid the traffic jams by staying for the *Kecak* dance and dinner, or leave quickly and finish the day at a stylish restaurant in the Petitenget/Seminyak area, such as **Chez Gado Gado** or **La Lucciola** (see pages 80–81).

Day 2: The Far South
Beaches, resorts & a cliff-top temple

Start before 10am to allow enough time to reach Ulu Watu by late afternoon. If staying in **Tanjung Benoa** or **Nusa Dua**, it is best to arrange your chartered/rented car the day before.

If starting early (before 8am) from the Kuta/Seminyak region or Sanur, a stop off at **Jimbaran** along the way is recommended. You could walk along the surprisingly undeveloped **beach**; explore one of Bali's best produce **markets**; or visit the 18th-century **Pura Ulun Siwi** temple, which is unusual because of its orientation towards Java and not Bali's Gunung Agung mountain.

A likable cross between the abrasiveness of Kuta and the sterility of Nusa Dua, **Tanjung Benoa** is a 5km (3.1 miles) stretch of beach along the extended "thumb" of Bukit Peninsula. Leave the car outside the quaint village at the northern tip and stroll around the fishing harbor and the admirable example of religious harmony: a Chinese temple, church, and mosque almost within a stone's throw of each other. The main attractions for most visitors, however, are on the water.

Only a few kilometers south is **Nusa Dua**, a gated complex of four- and five-star resorts with features unheard of elsewhere in southern Bali: wide footpaths, minimal traffic, and zero hawkers. Clean (but sterile) and hassle-free (but lacking any atmosphere), Nusa Dua is like nowhere else in Indonesia. An attraction for some is hitting a little white ball with a long gray stick at the **Bali Golf & Country Club** (baligolfandcountryclub.com), but do try to visit the **Museum Pasifika** (Blok P, 10am–6pm daily) art gallery with its inspiring array of works from Bali, Indonesia, and

Pura Luhur Ulu Watu sits on a spectacular cliff edge.

the Asia-Pacific region. You may want to finish off the morning abusing your credit card or having lunch at the **Bali Collection** mall (see page 87) or sun-worshipping along the public beach between the two headlands.

The only attraction in the dry, scrubby interior of the bulbous Bukit Peninsula is the massive **Garuda Wisnu Kencana Cultural Park** (9am–10pm daily), which has been under development for more than 20 years. Featuring souvenir shops, restaurants, cultural shows every hour from 11am, and a gigantic statute of Vishnu, surprisingly it's not nearly as tacky as it sounds.

Along the far southern coastline are a number of cliff-top luxury resorts, such as Bulgari and Banyan Tree. All offer sophisticated dining with sublime views, and a few even have small private beaches with restaurants open to the public and only accessible by dramatic elevators, such as Karma Kandara (karmakandara.com).

The western coastline is dotted with cliffside surfing beaches, but most are only accessible down unstable steps from isolated roads. The easiest on the eye and to reach is **Padang-Padang** (also known as Labuhan Sait), which has pure-white sand, plenty of shade, and cheap *warung* serving basic food. But don't linger too long: make sure you're at the revered cliff-top temple

of **Pura Luhur Ulu Watu** by 4pm to allow enough time to finish the day at Jimbaran, famed for its seafood dinners on the beach. You would've missed eating during sunset (it's the same one at Ulu Watu!), but many of the crowds would have disappeared by about 8pm. Along the row of cafés at Kedonganan (in the northern stretch), you can enjoy fireworks and wandering musicians; some cafés also offer *Legong* dances.

Day 3: **Sanur & Denpasar**
An older resort area with village charm

What makes Sanur really special is the **beachside promenade** lined with cafés, shops, and hotels that stretches more than 5km (3.1 miles) from north of Jalan Hang Tuah to where the mangroves take over in the south. Exploring this path and the village to the west in a full loop on foot will take five to six hours (not including stops), but **cycling** (one hour, plus stops) is not only possible but an absolute joy, even along the main streets (except the Bypass Road). Bikes are easy to rent.

Start along the promenade at the end of Jalan Hang Tuah, where there's a "port" (but no jetty) for speedboats and public boats to Nusa Lembongan. The multi-storey **Inna Grand Bali Beach** hotel horrified local

Fishing boats on Sanur Beach

elders so much that building restrictions were immediately introduced to prohibit further construction anywhere on Bali higher than a palm tree. (Recent development seems to be flouting these regulations, however.) The **Museum Le Mayeur** (8am–4pm Sat–Thurs; 8.30am–12.30pm Fri) houses distinctive works by one of Sanur's earliest foreign settlers, the Belgian artist Adrien Le Mayeur, but the beachside gardens are more appealing.

The promenade continues south past numerous beachside cafés, souvenir markets, and classy hotels until mangroves replace the sand at **Pura Mertasari** temple. Head back inland along the main road (not too busy) which starts as Jalan Merta Sari and eventually becomes Jalan Danau Tamblingan. At Regina Tailors (near the incongruously undeveloped jungle opposite the Bali Hyatt), turn left and explore the village and villas along Jalan Kesari, Bumi Ayu and then Pungutan, which leads to the produce **market**. Continue along Jalan Danau Toba and use the delightful shortcut between the golf course and Inna Grand hotel that passes a rare **mosque** and finishes where you started.

If you have time, some other attractions are not far away by taxi. **Bali Orchid Gardens** (baliorchidgardens. com; 8am–6pm daily) are a haven of tropical foliage intertwined with shady walkways. **Pulau Serangan** (known as

"Turtle Island") was once slated for development but is still quiet and ideal for cycling (but this would involve pedalling along the Bypass Road for about 4km/2.5 miles to get there). On the island are the revered **Pura Sakenan** temple, and the **Turtle Conservation & Education Center** with pools full of cute little critters designed to educate local school children. Impressively laced with walkways, the extensive **Mangrove Center** (9am–5pm daily) is a welcome respite from the traffic and heat, but also more focussed on education than tourism.

After a leisurely lunch at one of those lovely beachside cafés you spotted along the promenade, hail a taxi to Bali's capital. Like most Indonesian cities, **Denpasar** is chaotic and polluted, but paradoxically it's part of the *real* "real Bali," where maybe 500,000 live, work and, somehow, breathe. Start at the captivating and frenzied **markets** (before they start winding down mid-afternoon) which offer cheaper alternative shopping to the normal art markets and malls (see page 87). The **Museum Negeri Propinsi Bali** (8am–4pm Sat–Thurs; 8.30am–12.30pm Fri) was opened in 1930 by artists concerned about the disintegration of Balinese culture and art. While the gardens are appealing, the exhibits, including archeological artefacts and a model of Borobudur temple are not why the museum was originally created, and many visitors find it underwhelming. But the immediate area is worth exploring, especially the **Taman Puputan** park opposite and the **Pura Agung Jagnatha** temple next door.

Then head back to Sanur to relish some grilled seafood at the community-run **Sanur Beach Market Bar & Restaurant** (see page 81) along the promenade, followed by toe-tapping sophistication at the **Jazz Bar & Grille** (see page 91).

Which southern beaches are best?

The sea at **Kuta** may look ideal for swimming, but the waves can be massive and undercurrents surprisingly strong. You absolutely *must* swim between the flags, where lifeguards wait for inevitable mishaps. Because of the waves, watersports are very limited. **Legian** also has dumpers, so it's not ideal for swimming (and there are fewer lifeguards), but it is more appealing for sunbathing because fewer surfboard rental shacks and makeshift massage tables occupy the sand.

In **Seminyak**, the waves are still strong, the beach becomes grayish and there are fewer lifeguards and surfers, but a definite drawcard are the handful of bean bag cafés on the sand. The beach at **Petitenget** is still wide but the sand is even grayer. The waves are just as menacing (with almost no flags or lifeguards) and beachside facilities are limited to a couple of *warung* (food stalls).

In **Sanur**, the sea is calm, so all types of watersports are available, but not so at low tide. The best places to bellow on a banana boat or panic while parasailing are Cemara Beach and at the end of Jalan Duyung. The nicest stretches of sand front the upmarket hotels and restaurants, while public beaches at the end of the access roads tend to be scruffy.

Swimming is wonderful at **Tanjung Benoa** because in some places breakwaters create small, protected curves of white sand, and outer reefs also negate the waves. But for many, it's all about water sports, which can be organized at a dozen places only 100m (109yds) from the main road; just turn up and jump on/in/up. Every conceivable activity is offered, so some of the shoreline, especially on weekends, seems as clogged with jet skis and banana boats as Jalan Legian (Kuta) is with taxis and trucks. Well, almost….

A modest selection of watersports is available at **Nusa Dua**, but this region is more about lying by the pool and turning crispy-red. The beaches are superb, including the exceptional public beach between the two headlands, each with a temple and shaped like islands (hence the name "Nusa Dua" which means "two islands.") Sadly, the public beach at Geger has now been desecrated by the highly-controversial construction of another mega-resort.

Parts of the white-sand crescent bay at **Jimbaran** are lined with boats, so the best beaches are near The Four Seasons resort and at the end of Jalan Pemelisan Agung. Jimbaran is comparatively empty, except when the masses start arriving from 5pm for the famed sunset dinner. Very limited watersports are available.

Not far south off Jimbaran, **Padang-Padang** is spectacular and popular (for surfers mostly), but there's nowhere to stay, and it takes an hour to get there from most hotels.

Padang-Padang Beach

Nusa Dua Beach

EXPLORING UBUD
Experience the cultural and spiritual heart of Bali

See Ubud inset on the folded map

The island's heart and soul, and the geographical center of southern Bali, can seem to offer almost too much at times: rice field walks and traditional dances to relish, art museums and galleries to explore, cooking courses and yoga classes to join, and traditional markets and villages to discover. And with a multitude of other attractions nearby, and proximity to the volcanoes in the central highlands and beaches along the eastern and southern coasts, many use Ubud as their only base in Bali. Popularity has its downside, however: parts of Ubud are bursting at the seams, and facilities are often inadequate—car parking is very limited and public transport only reaches as far as Gianyar and Denpasar.

Day 1: Ubud Village
So much to see ... so little time

The logical point to commence this exploratory walking tour of Ubud is the *pasar umum*. This **public market** is a mesmerizing place to bargain over T-shirts or tea leaves, bananas or bangles, at stalls and from old ladies surrounded by baskets sprawled across the ground—although the atmosphere has changed somewhat with the recent construction of a new market building. Start before 8am when the rambling mass of produce mostly disappears as the souvenir stalls take over.

Directly opposite the market is **Ubud Palace**, also known as **Puri Saren Agung** (permanently open). As a palace (*puri*) rather than a temple (*pura*), non-Hindus are welcome to wander about and admire the architecture, but try to resist playing the *gamelan* instruments laying idle in anticipation for the evening's traditional performance. Across the side-road (Jalan Suweta) is a **wantilan**, a huge open-aired pavilion used for village meetings and as a rest stop for weary tourists. Continuing down the main road (Jalan Raya Ubud) is the **Pura Dalem Ubud** temple, closed to non-Hindus but easy to admire from the outside. The next stop is **Pura Taman Saraswati**, a majestic temple at the back of a pond choked with lotus flowers, and the ideal spot to experience a traditional dance (see page 17). The magnificent **Museum Puri Lukisan** close by features an outstanding collection of works created by local artists and foreigners inspired by Bali (see page 101).

A little further down the main road are the starting points for two of the best **walks** on the island: "Abangan"

Puri Saren Agung, also known as Ubud Palace

(1½ hour loop) and "Campuhan Ridge" (two hours return)—see pages 112-113 for details. Mostly flat and shady, and always inspiring, both walks finish more or less where they begin. By now you'll need some respite and sustenance, so a minute further down Jalan Raya Ubud is **Murni's Warung** restaurant, nestled alongside a ravine and adjacent to a delightful wooden bridge (see page 82).

A few hundred meters down from Murni's some obvious steps lead up to **Penestanan**. Sadly, some of the verdant rice fields tourists want to see have now been demolished to build bungalows tourists want to occupy, but the tranquil setting still lends itself to being the spiritual center of Ubud. Spend an hour or more meandering past **yoga** and **meditation** centers, private villas, and organic cafés along trails sometimes barely more than the edges of *subak* aqueducts used for rice field irrigation. Keep walking through Penestanan until the far (western) road, then turn right for an immediate taste of village life, or continue straight past Café Vespa for another 500m (546yds) to the main road at Sayan. Five-star resorts along the ridge at **Sayan** charge the earth for villas with views of the Ayung River, but with a little cheek you could walk down through the car park of a resort like The Four Seasons for **views** of Bali's longest and most voluminous river.

Now find an *ojek* (motorbike taxi), or walk back through Penestanan to the main road (Jalan Raya Ubud) and walk 1.4km (0.87 miles) up past the Bintang Supermarket to the **Neka Art Museum**, with its marvellous artworks and lush gardens (see page 101). Then perhaps finish your exhausting day with dinner, drinks and a dance at the **Jazz Café Tebesaya** (see page 91).

Door guardians stand at the entrance to the Monkey Forest.

Day 2: **Around Ubud**
Monkeys, pigs, art, and rice fields

In the morning finish off the highlights of Ubud on foot, at lunchtime "pig out" on roast pig (*babi guling*), and enjoy some flora and fauna during the afternoon and early evening (for which you'll need a chartered/rented car or motorbike, or bicycle). Start earlier than 9am, before the bus crowds arrive and the banana-snatching residents get too pesky, at the **Sacred Monkey Forest Sanctuary**, a lush jungle with eerie temples at the edge of Ubud's urban sprawl (see page 19 for more details).

Accessible along a path (800m/ 870yds) from the car park at the Monkey Forest (and through the southern gate) is **Nyuhkuning**, a charming village renowned for its wood carvings. Admirably undeveloped (thus far), and only dotted with a few inviting mid-priced bungalows and open-air cafés, the flat road is ideal for **cycling** (with bikes also available for rent). Follow the delightful road (1.5km/1 mile) south through Nyuhkuning and the busier thoroughfare east (1.1km/0.7 miles) to the magnificent **Agung Rai Museum of Art** (see page 101 for more details). Maybe pause for a drink/muffin at the café before wandering about the expansive collection and flourishing gardens.

Staying in Ubud

The crisp air, views and *padi* fields are highly conducive to **walking** (see Best Walks in Chapter 3). Pedestrian-friendly villages include Penestanan and Nyuhkuning, while two flat roads with minimal traffic also worth exploring on foot are Jalan Kaleng and Jalan Bisma, which connects (just) to the bottom of Monkey Forest Road. Much of the potential pleasure of **cycling** is affected by ravines, Kuta-esque traffic and annoyingly bumpy roads, but four places are pedal-worthy: (1) Petulu (although it's a busy road and you'll need lights coming back after watching the birds); (2) the botanical gardens (along a flat but bumpy road); (3) Goa Gajah and Yeh Pulu (see pages 45–46); and (4) Nyuhkuning.

Bali's cultural capital is home to a plethora of private **galleries** and several outstanding **art museums**, many of which are worth visiting just for their sumptuous gardens, often with cafés overlooking lotus-filled ponds. The very best places to see and buy arts and crafts are listed in the art & crafts section on page 89. At the risk of further cultural overload, watching at least one **traditional performance** of dance or music is almost obligatory. The variety of shows and the number of locations on offer may seem overwhelming, so we've provided some descriptions of what to see and suggestions about where to go (see pages 110–111). If you still have time left after all that, consider doing a short course in language, cooking or arts & crafts. Much on offer can be over-priced and underwhelming, so the very best courses are described on pages 107–109.

Phew! With all that mental and visual stimulation, you'll probably need to relax. Ubud is the epicenter in Bali, Indonesia and, most probably, Southeast Asia for **yoga**, **meditation** and **traditional healing**, although the usual types of massages and spas are also on offer. More details on where to improve your physical, spiritual, and emotional well-being are on pages 105–106.

Botanic Garden, Ubud

Goa Gajah, Ubud

From the ARMA museum, head north up the road that soon turns into **Jalan Hanoman**. With jewelry stores, fine-art galleries, and clothing boutiques, this street offers the best shopping in Ubud (see pages 87–88). At Jalan Raya Ubud, head left (west) and follow the signs up Jalan Suweta for a lunch of succulent roast pig at **Ibu Oka** (see page 82).

During the afternoon, visit two places that showcase the region's flora and bird-life. **Botanic Garden in Ubud** (botanic-gardenbali.com; 8am–6pm daily), a gentle 2.5km (1.5 miles) stroll up from Jalan Raya Ubud, attracts conservationists and hobby-gardeners for its orchid house, cacti patch, ponds, and rainforest, as well as fruit and herbal gardens. Sadly, it has declined in recent years, evinced by the closure of the quaint garden café.

Nearly 50 years ago, for reasons unknown, thousands of herons and egrets (collectively known in Balinese as *koko-kan*) started flocking to a few selected trees along the main street of **Petulu**. With admirable entrepreneurial spirit, this has now become a tourist attraction. Just turn up between 4pm and 5pm and watch the trees blossom with white feathers from a poop-proof drink stall among the *padi* fields. About 3.5km (2.1 miles) north from Ubud market, Petulu is most accessible by *ojek* or taxi; either will wait and bring you back for a convivial dinner at **Bali Buddha** (see page 82).

Day 3: East of Ubud
Caves, springs and rock shrines

Now it's time to escape the urbanization of Ubud. This excursion is also certainly possible by *bemo* (public transport) or even bicycle (but not to Sebatu and Tegallalang, which are too far). From the Ubud market, catch any *bemo* towards Gianyar and get off at Goa Gajah; then take another from the junction in Bedulu (near Yeh Pulu) to Tampaksiring. Aim to be at Goa Gajah before the bus hordes start arriving at 9am.

Goa Gajah (7am–6pm daily) is mysterious and irresistibly fascinating. It's mostly known for the small T-shaped cave created over 1,000 years ago that contains Hindu and Buddhist artefacts and some of the earliest identified examples of Balinese inscriptions. The bizarre carvings around the entrance may have given the cave its unusual name (no elephants ever existed in Bali), although that is debatable. Within the complex are shrines, a pool (not for swimming or bathing), and the usual *banjar* open-air pavilion. Steepish steps at the back of the *banjar* lead down to **Arca Buddha**, an unspectacular little temple positioned among attractive ponds and waterfalls. And you don't need a guide, despite what you may be told at the main entrance.

Gunung Kawi, with its pools, springs, and gardens

At the T-junction about 600m (650yds) past Goa Gajah, veer right towards Gianyar to find the turn-off to **Yeh Pulu**. This 25m (82ft) long series of 2m (6.5ft) high rock carvings dating back to the 14th century is reasonably impressive, but the enchanting path (a flat 600m/ 650yds) from the car park is more appealing. This area (including around **Samuan Tiga**) is ideal for **cycling**.

An obvious turn-off in Tampaksiring leads to **Gunung Kawi**, where massive shrines are carved into cliffs surrounded by stunning landscapes (see the special section on page 20). Not far down from the beginning of the imposing series of steps to the shrines is **Kafe Kawi**, the perfect place for lunch.

About 1km (0.62 miles) further up Tampaksiring is **Tirta Empul** (8am– 6pm daily), an immaculate complex of pools, temples, and gardens. The hot water springs are regarded as the holiest in Bali and (apparently) have the magical powers to heal 30 mental and physical ailments, so this is one of the most visited places on the island—by locals, not foreigners. As a result, it's *very* busy on Sundays and during a full moon, and while possible to splash about in the spring-fed pool, there's no privacy

and you may be sharing it with hundreds of others. The road just before the entrance to Tirta Empul leads to **Manca-wara Palace**, built by Indonesia's founding father, President Soekarno (whose mother was Balinese). The palace is now home to **The Soekarno Center** (sukarnocenter.com), with statues, photos, and various memorabilia dedicated to the remarkable man.

Head west from the Tirta Empul junction in Tampaksiring to Sebatu, where there's another enticing (and often ignored) collection of pools, springs, and gardens, also inexcusably called **Gunung Kawi**. From there, ask directions to **Kendaran**—with sloping coconut palms flanked by *padi* fields and volcano silhouettes, this is one of the most scenic roads in Bali. At the end of the road near Petulu, turn north to **Tegallalang**, a village with an inordinate number of handicraft shops. This road eventually opens up to reveal a series of chiselled rice terraces fronted by cafés with names like Rice Terrace Café. (Thankfully, these restaurants are better at cooking dinners than choosing names.) Then it's time to return for that quintessential Ubud experience: a traditional dance performance with live music.

*Also see Padangbai, Amed, and Tulamben
insets on the folded map*

Eastern Bali boasts a number of attractive beaches, elegant water palaces, mighty volcanoes, scenic back roads, and enchanting villages. It does not, however, offer surf, nightclubs, and shopping, which is why the region is also refreshingly quiet. But this is changing as road improvements make this region more accessible from the southern beaches, and those who shuttle to/from Lombok and the Gili Islands are slowly realizing the virtues of also basing themselves here.

Day 1: **The Road East**
To scenic Padangbai and Candidasa

Spend the morning traipsing around a temple and traditional village, the afternoon at a secluded beach and the evening revelling in Bali's Happiest Hours. Start this excursion at about 9am; two hours earlier if you want to explore Padangbai beforehand.

Padangbai is beginning to blossom as a tourist destination in its own right, rather than just a place to jump on a ferry to Lombok or speedboat to the Gili Islands (see page 12). The village isn't bustling with heaps of attractions, which is unquestionably part of the charm, but Padangbai is a more appealing base than Candidasa (which has no real

beach) and Amed (which is remote). Refer to page 23 for more details.

Along the road back towards the southern beaches is **Pura Goa Lawah**, the "Bat Cave Temple" (8am–7pm daily), famous for the masses of hideous creatures that lurk at the entrance to a cave at the back of the complex. According to legend, the cave stretches up to 20km (12.4 miles) inside Mount Agung and is inhabited by a dragon—but perhaps that story is a little too batty? But with its magnificent *meru* shrines, Goa Lawah is one of the oldest and holiest temples on the island and home to frequent (and usually vast) ceremonies. The seaside setting with views across to Nusa Penida is also photogenic.

On the way to Candidasa is the turn-off to **Tenganan** (8am–5.30pm daily), the best example of a Bali Aga village. This means the village predates the introduction of Hinduism and inhabitants still practice unique ancient traditions about, for example, marriage and cremation. Tenganan is a fascinating museum of real life, almost medieval in its setting, with congenial residents and a refreshing mountain backdrop. From the entrance, simply amble along one stony laneway past **weaving workshops** and **souvenir stalls** to the end (at the school) and stroll back down the parallel path. Between the two thoroughfares are a series of *banjar* pavilions used for meetings, storage and per-

Pleasure boats moored at the beach at Padangbai.

formances and plenty of caged roosters primed for cock-fighting. Other **paths** nearby are residential, but more authentic and worthy of exploration.

The major industry is now producing and selling souvenirs, of course, but the superb range and quality make this village Bali's most unique shopping experience (see page 88). Tenganan is a place to savor, not rush, so chat to locals, watch them weave, wander around the outer paths and venture into the countryside. Tenganan is at the end of a delightful, flat road (3.3km/2 miles) that starts just before Candidasa. If you fancy a walk, take an *ojek* (motorbike taxi) there from the turn-off and return on foot, but time your visit so you can enjoy lunch at the **Candi Bakery**, only 200m (218yds) up from the turn-off. It offers drinks (including wine), scrumptious cakes, and a variety of Dutch- and Indonesian-style meals in a charming setting.

A few kilometers past Candidasa is **Pasir Putih**, one of the most alluring beaches in Bali, just a short walk (1.5km/ 1 mile) from the main road. This crescent bay of rare white sand is more of a fishing village than a tourist beach and delightfully undeveloped (so far); in fact, it's worthy of a special section (see page 14).

After splashing about, snorkeling around and slurping coconut juice at Pasir Putih, return to Candidasa, which is a beach resort without a beach. Decades ago, reefs were destroyed to make cement for the construction of new hotels and the shore disappeared. A few snatches of sand have been recreated by breakwaters, but there's no real beach for swimming, sunbathing, or even strolling. On the plus side, Candidasa is compact and easily accessible, and most hotels offer rooms with views of the sea and islets.

The main road is only 1.2km (0.74 miles) long, so park your car at the rocky **public**

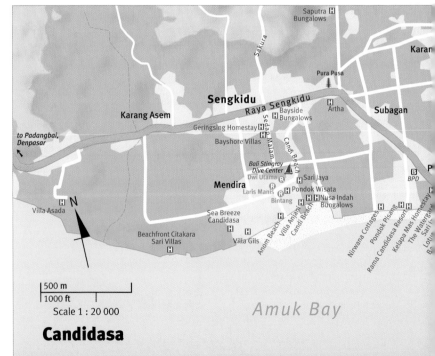

Candidasa

Scale 1 : 20 000

500 m
1000 ft

Amuk Bay

beach (opposite the police station) and go for a stroll. Near the far (eastern) end is the **Puri Candidasa** temple. Built over 500 years ago, it's undersized but better maintained than others, and the **views** are worth the short climb. Opposite is the **lagoon**, behind which boatmen laze about on a *bale* pavilion overlooking a miniscule beach. They (and a few agencies along the main road) offer **boat trips**, but it's hard to rustle up the minimum number of passengers required. **Scuba diving** is better organized in Padangbai, but **snorkeling** is still possible around the three endearing islets. The necessary equipment can be hired from the boatman.

Many of Candidasa's **restaurants** face the busy road, which means almost shouting at your dinner companion and breathing in fumes from cars, not aromas from food. A quieter spot to relish the breezes, photograph the islets and admire a rare pocket of sand is **Pandan**

Restaurant. There's a modicum of **nightlife**, but it's very tame compared to the southern beaches. But the perpetual dearth of tourists does mean extraordinary value: most restaurants offer *Legong* dances, live music, jolly happy hours, and very reasonable two/three-course set-priced meals.

Day 2: **Amlapura to Amed**
Circling Bali's far eastern coast

Starting in Amlapura at about 8am will allow you time to fully explore the far eastern coast (including a leisurely lunch at Amed), as well as Tirtagangga and the surrounding region, and maybe finish there with drinks, a meal and an overnight stay.

Amlapura, the capital of the once-mighty kingdom of Karangasem, is now famous for the **Puri Agung Karangasem** palace (8am–5pm daily). This small complex built by the Dutch in the late 18th century is

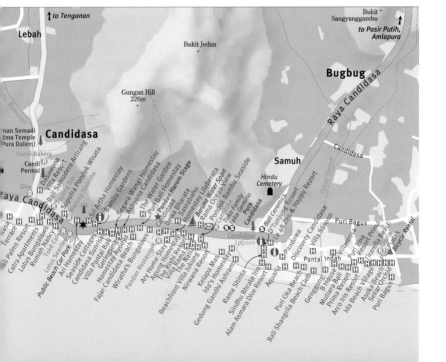

The Taman Soeksada water palace at Ujung

noteworthy for its design with a mixture of Balinese, Chinese, Javanese, and European influences. These are particularly evident in the Bale Maskerdam pavilion, which contains photos and furniture depicting Balinese and Dutch life during colonial times, and the Bale Kambang, a smaller version of the "Floating Pavilion" at the palace in Semarapura. Across the road, the **Puri Gede** palace has been renovated and is worth checking out. To explore the rest of the town, including the **market** 500m (546yds) further south, leave your car at the palace and walk.

Taman Soeksada Ujung water palace (7am–6pm daily) is accessible by *ojek* (motorbike taxi) or strolling (3km/1.8 miles) downhill from the Amlapura market. Always a bridesmaid to those in Semarapura and Tirtagangga, this water palace was originally built by the local king in 1921 but obliterated in an earthquake about 40 years later, so only a small stained archway at the top of the hill remains. The palace has been completely rebuilt in recent years and now features an elegant series of bridges, pavilions, and lotus-filled ponds. There's too much cement and not enough vegetation, but it's hard to deny the majesty of the expansive setting under the watchful eye of Mount Agung.

Opposite, the rocky shore is lined with the sort of fishing vessels you'll notice along the road to Amed, which starts from the car park at Ujung palace. This glorious road squeezed between Mount Seraya and the cliffs along the far eastern coast is now fully paved. With its endearing fishing villages and scarred mountain terraces, this region offers landscapes and views like nowhere else on Bali.

Amed is one of several fishing villages along this coast, but also the generic name given to the 10km (6.2 miles) long stretch which includes other places like Bunutan, Lipah, and Jemeluk. This area really has only one purpose: **scuba diving** (but not snorkeling), which can be arranged at companies dotted along the road, such as Jukung Dive (jukungdive-bali.com). Much of the coastline is cliffs with villages nestled below, and the rare snatches of sand are mostly gray and rocky, and often difficult to access. The best **beach** is at the "clk 10" road marker in front of the Palm Garden Resort, but you'll still have to share the water's edge with dozens of *jukung* fishing boats.

There are plenty of picturesque restaurants to stop for lunch, such as **Sails** at **Bunutan** (see page 83), but maybe think twice before staying in Amed: there's no public transport (except for very occasional shuttle buses), nothing to do but scuba-dive, and everything is just *so* spread out. There are clusters of homestays and beachside cafés in the real Amed village around the "clk 4" and "clk 5" road markers, but Tirtagangga is a more likable alternative for an overnight stay. The road from Amed ends at the lifeless transport hub of Culik, from where a road heads left (south) and weaves past unexpectedly lush rice terraces to **Tirtagangga**. Bali's most exquisite water palace boasts a charming hotel with an elegant restaurant (but cheaper places to stay and eat are also nearby), and the dazzling sunset is free. Tirtagangga is so wonderful it deserves a special section (see page 15).

Day 3: Pura Besakih
A visit to Bali's "Mother Temple"

Pagodas rise over the landscape at Pura Besakih.

If you begin this leisurely excursion at around 10am, and then take your chartered/rented car along the scenic road to Pura Besakih via Sidemen, you can stop for lunch at one of a handful of appealing cafés 500m (546yds) down from the roundabout at Sidemen.

Semarapura was capital of a powerful kingdom for about 300 years, but is now best known for the **Puri Semarapura** water palace (7.30am–5pm daily), dedicated to the God of Love. Most of the palace was destroyed in 1908 by Dutch colonialists as hundreds of Balinese undertook a suicidal uprising (*puputan*) rather than surrender, but it has been mostly rebuilt and is now lovingly maintained. The Bale Kambang is surrounded by a moat choked with fish and therefore called "The Floating Pavilion." It features painted panels retelling traditional stories of love and peace, and other tales of astrological importance. In another corner of the complex is the **Kerta Gosa**, which served as the Hall of Justice. Again, you'll need to tilt your head upwards to truly appreciate the multi-layered (but much-altered) paintings about Javanese and Balinese legends. The **Museum Semarajaya** contains some artefacts, as well as weaving, sculptures, and explanations about the *puputan*.

Leave your car outside the palace and explore the town on foot for a taste of Balinese (with a touch of Chinese) urban life. Opposite the palace are the expansive public **market** (the best in the region) and the **Puputan Monument**, a memorial made from black volcanic rock with dioramas inside about local history. And another alluring temple, **Pura Taman Sari**, is 500m (546yds) northeast from the palace.

The Mother of all Temples is perched along the slopes of the Mother of all Mountains, Gunung Agung. **Pura Besakih** (9am–4pm daily) is a multitiered complex of 22 temples and dozens more pagodas and shrines spread across three square kilometers (740 acres), although the eye-popping setting is sometimes smothered by low clouds. Dating back to the 8th century, the temples were almost completely rebuilt after the 1917 earthquake, but amazingly they survived the brunt of Agung's anger during the eruption of 1963.

Non-Hindus aren't permitted inside the main temple, **Pura Penataran Agung**, or even climb steps to it without a guide, but you can still observe a fair bit from the stairway along the lefthand side. (All other temples are accessible.) Pura Besakih is exceptionally sacred and home to frequent ceremonies, especially during full moon, while the main event, the **Batara Turun Kabeh festival**, is held 10–20 days either side of the full moon in April or May.

The complex is at the end of a scenic road (5km/3 miles and uphill) from Menanga. To avoid a 500m (546yd) walk and the persistent souvenir stallholders, follow the road marked "Kintamani" to the very end and park there. If you're relying on public transport, you should be able to cadge a lift from Menanga. Just one warning: some visitors are rightly dismayed by the pushy hawkers and guides around the temples. Just try to grin and bear it.

EXPLORING BALI'S HIGHLANDS & NORTH COAST
Hot springs, crater lakes, waterfalls, and dolphins

Also see Lovina Beach inset on the folded map

Those lazing about the southern beaches often ignore this region because they think it's too far (but only three hours from Sanur to Lovina); there's nothing to see or do (absolutely incorrect); and there's no shopping and nightlife (well, those bits are right). And it is true that the beaches along Lovina are unappealing, but the north coast is ideal for anyone sick of the chaos down south. Many visit the volcanic regions of the central highlands on day trips or as quick stopovers on the way to Lovina, but opt to stay and soak up the cool weather while enjoying the views, water sports, hiking, and hot springs.

Day 1: Lake Bratan Area
As much fun on the lake as around it

Start with an exploration on foot of Candikuning before strolling down to Bedugul for a zip around the lake by speedboat before lunch. Then walk 2km (1.24 miles) back (or take a bus) and spend the rest of the day at the temple.

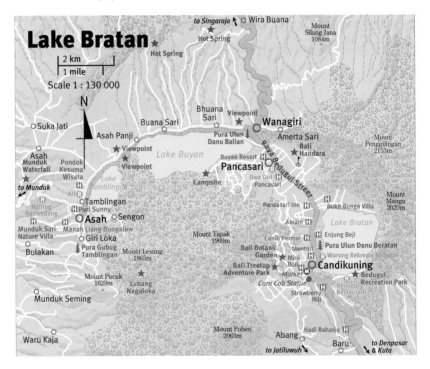

The best place for dinner is Warung Rekreasi Bedugul (opposite the market), probably the only place on Bali to offer (and need) a wood fire.

Candikuning has a sizable Muslim community, a **market** where day-trippers create traffic jams while stopping to buy corn, strawberries, or rabbits, and several places to stay and eat. Only 500m (546yds) from the landmark "Corn Cob Statue" is the immaculate, 160-hectare **Bali Botanic Garden** (balibotanic-garden.org; 7am–6pm daily). One of only four in Indonesia (and the largest), it's the perfect place to admire local flora, including orchids and the elusive Green Rose, and to escape the noise, heat and chaos of southern Bali. But avoid Sundays, when thousands of locals visit the gardens, particularly the **Bali Treetop Adventure Park** (see page 95).

At the southern end of the lake, an easy 20-minute walk down from Candikuning, is **Bedugul**, a lakeside recreation area so enticing it has its own special section (see page 10). The restaurant overlooking the lake is definitely worth stopping for lunch (see page 83).

One of Bali's most famous sights is unquestionably the **Pura Ulun Danu Bratan** temple (7am–7pm daily). Built over 350 years ago and dedicated to the Goddess of Lakes, it features immaculate waterside gardens and those *meru* shrines you've seen so often on postcards and Rp50,000 notes. Although the most sacred areas are closed to non-Hindus, there's still plenty to admire. The complex is most photogenic during late afternoon, when boys start fishing, the sun gleams off the *meru* shrines, and tour groups have returned south. Canoes and speedboats can be hired for better views (especially appealing early morning), but **boat trips** and other mild,

The lakeside temple of Pura Ulun Danu Bratan

Fishing vessels stand idle on Lake Bratan.

family-oriented water sports are cheaper just outside the entrance.

If you still have the energy you may want to explore the region further on foot. At the northern corner of the market in Pancasari, a flat road (3km/1.8 miles) leads to a simple but alluring campsite on the southern edge of **Lake Buyan**. Alternatively, take a *bemo* to the turn-off at Wanagiri and stroll as far as you want along the ridge to monkey-infested **lookouts** that offer views of the twin lakes of Buyan and Tamblingan and to the north coast from the other side.

Day 2: **Gunung Batukau**
Bali's second highest volcano

If you don't have private transport, ask at your hotel in Candikuning/Bedugul, or at travel agency stalls at the market, for a car with a driver, although an *ojek* is far

Pura Luhur Batukau

easier to arrange. Starting at about 10am will allow time for lunch at a café overlooking the rice terraces at **Jatiluwih** (which are so spectacular they deserve their own section—see page 18). From Jatiluwih, a series of potholes, occasionally connected with bitumen, leads to **Pura Luhur Batukau**, high on the slopes of Gunung Batukau (2,271m/ 7,450ft). This sacred former state temple is irresistibly serene and swathed from a verdant forest humming with insects and birds that surrounds an artificial lake. It's so inviting—despite the frequent signs informing visitors that entrance to the temple and mobile phones are strictly forbidden—but rarely visited.

Day 3: Gunung Batur
Views, buffets, springs, and hawkers

Everyone stops for the **views**, many scoff down a **buffet lunch**, a few swear at some hawkers and then almost everyone disappears, but there's so much more to explore inside the caldera. Starting in **Penelokan** at about 8am with a chartered/rented car allows you time to explore the crater rim during the morning, stroll alongside the lake, and then wallow about the hot springs in the afternoon. But remember: this is the coldest, wettest and foggiest part of any tourist region in Bali.

The first stop should be the surprisingly good **Museum Gunungapi Batur** (see page 102), which will provide the perfect introduction to, and explanation about, the Batur volcano. Optimum views (which include the mountain and lake) are about 2km (1.2 miles) east of Penelokan, along the road to Rendang. Sadly, many people's opinion of this area is soured by the constant hassling by **hawkers** selling souvenirs and postcards (remember those?). They're insatiable and will not take *tidak* for an answer. (Curiously, they're all swept aside when VIPs visit.)

Further around the rim, the **Pura Ulun Danu Batur** temple seems unexceptional at first sight, but features some 90 shrines dedicated to the very important God of Rice Irrigation. The complex is well set up for visitors, with tickets including entrance to a museum, sash/sarong hire,

Trekking on Batur

Scene of several eruptions (most recently in 2000), Gunung Batur (1,717m/ 5,633ft) is a dream for geologists and trekkers. Trekking is best arranged in Toya Bungkah through the monopolistic Association of Mt Batur Trekking Guides (0366-52362; 4am–4pm). This outfit charges like the proverbial wounded bull but there's no way around it, even if you book through a hotel. (Note: a guide here can make more for a half-day hike with four people than a school teacher earns in two weeks.) The easiest hike (3–4 hours) starts at 5am, while the toughest (7 hours) begins at 3am and is timed to witness the surreal sunrise at the peak.

The volcanic crater and lake of Mount Batur as seen from Penelokan

and guide. The crater-lipped thoroughfare continues through **Kintamani**, with some limited shops and the region's biggest **market**, and ends at **Penulisan**. The **Pura Puncak Penulisan** temple (1,745m/5,725ft) is the highest in Bali and provides astounding 360-degree views—cloud, mist and rain permitting.

It's a cliché, but lunch at one of the restaurants along **Penelokan** that cling to the crater rim with views of the lava-scarred slopes is recommended. Obviously, the fancier-looking places are more expensive but their buffets are more extensive.

From Penelokan, a steep, windy road descends to the main lakeside village, **Toya Bungkah**. Unlike Lake Bratan, Batur is inadequately set up for **boat trips**. The ticket office at Kedisan does offer boat rides to the traditional Bali

Aga village of **Trunyan**, but charges like the trekking guides: a 10-minute return trip costs about the same as hiring a car with a driver for eight hours.

Avoid this daylight robbery and **walk** instead. Unfortunately, paths don't hug the water's edge because this fertile land is more profitably used for growing vegetables. One option is the road (3.1km/ 1.9 miles) from Toya Bungkah to the picturesque village of **Songan**, from where it's only another 1.3km (0.8 miles) to **Pura Hulun Danu**, original site of the Pura Ulun Danu Batur temple before it was moved away from danger to Batur village. Alternatively, walk along the windy road (9km/5.6 miles) from Kedisan to Trunyan, via Abang, which is steep in patches but offers the finest **lake views**. To venture into that eerie black lava-land visible from the crater rim, continue along the road from Songan or start at a path that's only 500m (546yds) west of the T-junction leading to Toya Bungkah. But don't go too far: the road is atrocious (not suitable for vehicles) and barely discernible.

Finish the day floundering about the hot springs and cold-water pools at one of the lakeside resorts in Toya Bungkah (see page 22). Both resorts have restaurants, while plenty of other cafés are within walking distance around the village.

A roadside fruit stand in Kintamani

Staying in Lovina: Sunsets and dolphins

Because the collection of villages known as Lovina stretches for 10km (6.2 miles) along the north coast and, therefore, some hotels are remote, you should base yourself in one of three places: (1) **Anturan**, a 100m (109yd) long, dead-end road with the best village vibe but very limited facilities; (2) **Banyualit**, more developed with just enough facilities to satisfy, but fading in popularity; or (3) **Kalibukbuk**, with far more facilities than the other two combined, but still tranquil and amiable.

The sea along this coast is skating-rink flat and ideal for **swimming**—it's just a pity about the **beaches**. The gray and gritty sand can't be helped, but much of the coastline is dirty and lined with *jukung* fishing boats. The beaches at Anturan and Banyualit are deplorable, and most multi-star resorts facing the sea in Lovina don't even bother grooming their beaches, which is why so many places (including no-star homestays) have **swimming pools**. (If yours doesn't, you can splash about the pools at the Astina and Angkosa hotels in Kalibukbuk for a small fee.) The most appealing from a very poor selection of beaches is at the **Dolphin Statue**, between the ends of Kalibukbuk's only two streets.

But there is plenty of action offshore. Several companies in Kalibukbuk organize **scuba diving** trips, although it's always better to deal directly with a reputable outfit like Spice Dive (balispicedive.com). The shallow reefs along Lovina are OK for **snorkeling**, but you'll need to bring or buy your own gear and charter a boat, so best to organize something with a scuba diving company. The much-lauded **dolphin tours** are usually heaps of fun, but be prepared for disappointment (and starting at 6am): it's not uncommon for trips to be dolphin-free.

There are several stores that rent **bicycles**, but few areas to actually use them. The main road is a race-track for trucks, and most streets to the south are potholed and head high into the hills. However, Jalan Raya Kalibukbuk, which starts at Lovina's only traffic light and leads to Singaraja, is perfect: flat, paved, and almost traffic-free. The best **walks** are along the beach between Kalibukbuk and Banyualit, and around Banjar (see page 114).

Lovina's gray sand beaches are poorly tended but provide adequate swimming opportunities.

Dolphins can be sighted off Lovina.

Day 4: **Around Lovina**
Singaraja, Gitgit, and Banjar

Start early with a dolphin tour (see page 56) and then charter a car with a driver to explore Singaraja (driving around any Indonesian city yourself is not recommended). Enjoy lunch near Bali's grandest waterfalls, spend the afternoon exploring Banjar, and finish with a seafood dinner at a unique beachside *lesehan* restaurant (see page 83).

With wide streets, bearable traffic and interesting architecture, the former capital **Singaraja** is more worthy of exploration than Bali's current capital. The **old Dutch port** (Pelabuhan Buleleng) is lined with sad, dilapidated buildings, but is still fascinating to wander about for the outlandish **Independence Monument**, the **Chinese temple**, and the **restaurants** perched above the water. **Gedong Kirtya** is an uninspiring collection of manuscripts in a building that's often closed, but a path beside it leads to the far more noteworthy Puri Agung Singaraja (**Royal Palace of Singaraja**) on Jalan Gajah Mada (daylight hours, daily). The attractive buildings are cluttered with old furniture,

decorated with colonial-era photos, and positioned around delightful courtyards. Next door, the **Museum Buleleng** (9am–5pm; Sun–Fri) is dedicated to the life of the final King of the region and is as (un)interesting as it sounds.

Then head south up the main road and stop for lunch at Gitgit Restaurant opposite the entrance to the **Gitgit Waterfalls**. There are actually three falls, but the most impressive, and Bali's highest (35m/114ft), is near here. A 500m (546yds) long trail lined with souvenir stalls leads to these gushing falls which are, of course, more impressive in the wet season.

Later, head west past Lovina and spend the afternoon exploring **Banjar**, a village with **hot springs** and a charming **monastery** (see page 21). This area can also be explored on foot (see Best Walks on page 114).

The Gigit waterfalls are most impressive during the wet season.

EXPLORING THE NUSA ISLANDS
Nusa Lembongan, Nusa Penida, and Nusa Ceningan

See Nusa Lembongan inset on the folded map

The main island of Lembongan (and Ceningan) may not boast the array of idyllic beaches of the Bali mainland, but nor does it have hawkers or traffic congestion either. In fact, there's no shopping or nightlife, and getting around involves boats, bicycles, motorbikes, and old-fashioned foot power. Many love Nusa Lembongan and never want to leave, but for these same reasons others are disappointed. Nusa Penida has more infrastructure (i.e., roads and public transport), but is poorly developed (so far) for tourism. More genuine than the Gilis and most places on Bali, the main industry on these three islands is harvesting seaweed rather than milking tourists.

Day 1: Nusa Lembongan
Is this the "real Bali" of your dreams?

It's best to stay in one of two places. **Jungutbatu**, where most boats arrive, is a likeable village based around the **Pura Segara temple** with its magnificent banyan tree. More appealing places to stay and eat are along Jungutbatu beach 500m (546yds) further north, but although highly photogenic, especially during the fiery (pollution-free) sunsets, the beach isn't really suitable for swimming or even sunbathing because of the *jukung* fishing boats and sheets of drying seaweed. The second main option, **Mushroom Bay**, caters more for package-tour crowds who frolic along the lovely crescent-shaped beach enjoying Lembongan's best **swimming** and **sunbathing**.

To explore the island further you can charter an *ojek* (motorbike taxi) or rent a motorbike. (Rental agencies don't worry about "incidentals" like helmets, registration papers, or even license plates for one simple reason: there are no traffic police on the island.) But the best way to get

Fishing boats pepper the coast at Jungutbatu Beach, Nusa Lembongan.

Waves break at Dream Beach, Nusa Lembongan.

around is by **bicycle** (see page 16), although the interior is very hilly in places.

Lembongan can be explored on foot, but walking around the entire island will take all day. Start early (before 8am) to avoid the heat, relax at lunchtime at a beachside café with a pool and spend the afternoon lazing about Mushroom Bay. Follow the advice and directions given for cyclists (see page 16), but note that walkers can detour around the monster hill between Lembongan village and Jungutbatu by scrambling (30 minutes) across rocks and sand from Mushroom Bay via the beaches of Selegimpak (also called Tamarind) and **Sanglambung**.

Walking clockwise, your first stop will be **Mangrove Beach**, where there are far more mangroves than beach, and plenty of *warung* offering food, drinks, snorkeling gear rental and **boat trips**. Another place to stop and rest is the rickety, wooden suspension bridge to **Nusa Ceningan**. This island is rugged, with very poor roads, but popular with surfers who flock to the protective outer reefs that delight both them and the seaweed farmers. A *warung* west of the bridge on

Lembongan offers extraordinary views of the seaweed farms that dominate these vast shallow waters.

The next stop is the T-junction in the other main village, **Lembongan**, where steps lead to a temple with fine views. Now it's time for lunch, so detour to **Sunset Beach** for The Beach Club at Sandy Bay (see pages 83-84); or the Dream Beach Huts at **Dream Beach**, with a cliff-top pool and the best bar-counter views in Bali (and much research was done on this topic). These two beaches are gorgeous to look at but terrifying to swim in because of strong currents and pounding waves, so finish the day lazing about **Mushroom Bay**. If you wine or dine there at any of the lovely seaside cafés during the evening, charter a boat or *ojek* back to Jungutbatu.

Day 2: Nusa Penida
This island may be the Next Big Thing

Arid, rugged, and surprisingly undeveloped for tourism, the former penal colony of Penida is slowly changing as speedboats now zip across every day

Getting to the Nusa Islands

How you reach Nusa Lembongan depends on what's more important: comfort, safety, speed, or cost. Between Sanur and Lembongan, Perama (peramatour.com) is the best value, while others, such as Scoot (scootcruise.com) and Rocky (rockyfastcruise.com), are quicker and more comfortable—and the former continues to Gili Trawangan. (Note: Perama drops off and collects passengers at Jungutbatu beach, where most people stay, while the other boat companies dock in Jungutbatu village 500–800m/546–870yds further south.) Crowded public boats (45 minutes) link Jungutbatu (Lembongan) with Toyapakeh (Penida) every morning but aren't timed for day trips. Penida is opening up with speedboats directly from Sanur operated by Maruti Express (balimarutiexpress.com) and Caspla (baliseaview.com). But remember: seas are always rough and none of these boats use jetties, so you'll have to wade through water (although someone will carry your luggage if need be).

from Sanur. But transport from Lembongan is not designed for day-tripping tourists, so you'll have to stay at least one night on Penida or charter a boat back to Nusa Lembongan. Two villages offer basic places to stay and eat: **Toyapakeh**, where most boats from Lembongan and Sanur arrive; and **Sampalan**, near the harbor used by slow public boats from Padangbai. Traveling around Penida takes time because roads are potholed and steep, and transport (except between the two villages) is limited to renting a motorbike or chartering a *bemo* or *ojek*. To minimize the hassle, perhaps join an **organized tour** from Sanur (see page 108).

There are three highlights: **Ped**, home to the **Pura Penataran Agung Ped** temple, set in a pond and greatly revered by worshippers from as far as mainland Bali; **Gua Karang Sari cave** (also called **Giri Putri**), more of a tunnel (200m/218yds long) and venerated by Buddhists and Hindus; and **Crystal Bay**, a postcard-worthy beach that would be crammed with villas if it was on Bali. Along the way, you may want to stop at the occasional **weaving workshop** and admire the cliff-top **views** across to the mainland.

Water sport activities on the Nusa Islands

Those massive *things* spoiling your views are **pontoons** and mega-jumbo-boats on which day-trippers (including families) from Bali revel in a mass of water-based activities (see page 95). **Surfers** are well catered for, but access to the best breaks usually involves chartering a boat from Jungutbatu, while **scuba diving** agencies such as World Diving (world-diving.com) offer trips to view the unique reefs and marine life around all three islands. **Snorkeling** is excellent (with gear available for rent) at Mushroom Bay and Mangrove Beach, and the usual array of **water sports** are available at the former. But whether you're under the water or on top of it, please note: currents are always strong and waves often dangerous.

EXPLORING WESTERN LOMBOK
The Gili Islands and Senggigi are a more rustic version of Bali

See Gili Islands and Senggigi Beach insets on the folded map

This part of Lombok has long tried to compete with the beaches and islands of its more renowned big sister to the west. But as one star continues to shine (the Gili Islands), another may possibly fade (Senggigi) as Lombok's only airport relocates from the appealing capital of Mataram, only a few kilometers from Senggigi, to near a sublime series of beaches along the southern coast in and around another place called Kuta.

Day 1: The Gili Islands
Three versions of paradise

To visit all three islands in one day, you'll have to charter a boat from at least one island to another. Assuming you stay on Gili Trawangan, take the morning public boat at about 9am to Gili Meno, and explore that island before chartering a boat to Gili Air, where you can enjoy lunch at an adorable beach-side café like **Gita Gili** (see page 84). Then take the afternoon public boat at around 4pm (or charter again) in time for a late afternoon exploration of Gili T. This can be followed by dinner at **Café Gili Trawangan** (see page 84) and late-night revelry at the **Tir Na Nog** nightclub (see page 92).

In stark contrast to Gili T, **Gili Meno** is a party-free zone. There's so much more time and space here, and when those boisterous day-trippers from Gili T return to "civilization" each afternoon, Gili M reverts back from just being sleepy to virtually comatose. There isn't much to do but **snorkel** and snooze, but that's part of the attraction and most of the charm. You can **walk** around the smallest of the Gilis in 75 minutes, but the sandy paths make **cycling** impossible (and no bikes are offered for rent anyway). The **Gili Meno Bird Park** (balipvbgroup.com; open 7.30am–12pm

Cafes line the beachfront on Gili Air.

Staying on the Gili Islands

The Gili Islands are understandably one of Indonesia's major attractions but their location, popularity, and size mean there are some things you should know. There are no **banks**; only a few **ATMs** on Gili Trawangan and one on Gili Air, although each island has **moneychangers**. **Blackouts** are not uncommon and only upmarket places have back-up generators. During **peak seasons** (July–August and mid-December to late-January), hotel prices can double and finding a room is difficult, so book ahead. The well **water** used in most guesthouses is a little malodourous, but OK for showering (not drinking, though bottled water is cheap), and the "fresh water" on offer at other places is really tap water imported from Lombok at great expense. And street lights? Well, there are no streets, so carry a **flashlight** at night.

A *cidomo* horse and cart on Gili Trawangan

Boat trips can be arranged on each island, but the choice of **water sports** is surprisingly limited. **Scuba diving** is easy to organize, but stick to reputable companies like Manta Dive (manta-dive.com) and Blue Marlin (bluemarlindive.com), and the **snorkeling** is so superb that we've dedicated a special section to it (see page 24). But remember: the best place to arrange any activity on or below the water is the more developed island, Gili Trawangan. Some **beaches** are lined with rocks and seaweed, so some recommended spots to lay down your towel and get sand wedged between your toes are in the following pages.

There's one **public boat** from one island to another each morning and afternoon, so it's only possible to day trip to one island (not two) from the one you're staying on. Buy tickets as soon as possible on the day of departure from the offices (open 7am–4.30pm daily) at the boat landings. **Chartering** boats is possible, but fares are fixed and high. The same can be said for the only public transport, the *cidomo* horse and cart, whose non-negotiable fares are about 10 times more per 500m (546yds) than metered taxis on Bali. Pay up or keep walking—but watch where you step.

Many companies offer **speedboats**, but most only go to/from Gili Trawangan. From Amed, Kuda Hitam (kudahitamexpress.com) travels to all three islands; and from Sanur, Scoot (scootcruise.com) also has connections to Nusa Lembongan and Gili Air. But the most common departure point is Padangbai, with the likes of Blue Water Express (bluewater-express.com) and Gili Cat (gilicat.com). To venture to the Lombok mainland, catch a public boat (which leaves when full) and endure the semi-organized chaos at the transport hub of Bangsal. The distance between the boat landing and bus terminal is 500m (546yds), but the only way to find your bus and its departure point is to pay (Rp10,000–15,000) for an annoyingly persistent *cidomo* driver to take you.

and 2–5.30pm daily) is worth a sticky-beak for its macaws, toucans, lonely crocodile and, of course, a museum dedicated to The Beatles. More birdlife can be spotted along a walkway that skirts the edge of the **salt lake**, while the **Turtle Sanctuary** (permanently open) is smaller but more informative than the one on Gili T. The best **beaches** are opposite the Kontiki Cottage and Malia's Child hotels.

Fitting oh-so-snugly between boozy Gili T and snoozy Gili M, **Gili Air**—which is pronounced *ay-airrr* and actually means "water" in Indonesian—has a genuine village vibe. Despite more regular connections to Lombok and Bali, Gili A is still pleasingly undeveloped, with prime **beach** frontage still being used to build boats, graze cows and, sadly, dump rubbish. The sea is calmer and the **beaches** are easy to spot from the path; **swimming** is especially good in front of Scallywags restaurant. A **stroll** around the island takes 90 minutes, and with better paths than the other two islands, and paved walkways

around the village, **cycling** is great fun (and bikes are easy to rent).

Then it's back to Gili T. Circling the island on **foot** takes about two hours, plus extra time for an obligatory beer, or three, at a "sunset bar" along the west coast. By **bicycle**, it takes about 45 minutes, although some sandy sections will test your pedaling prowess. Along the way is the **Turtle Conservation Center** (giliecotrust.com; permanently open), home to a few cute little *penyu* anxiously waiting to be released. Most paths heading inland are now paved, which makes exploring the village easier, while a steepish path to **Sunset View Point** offers superb Gili-ramas. The best **beaches** are in front of the major hotels—e.g. Villa Armika and Alam Gili, both along the shady north coast.

Day 2: Senggigi Beach
Lombok's premier beach resort area

The long sweep of crescent-shaped beaches known collectively as

Senggigi Beach consists of a series of sandy coves ideal for swimming and sunbathing.

Senggigi is vastly different to the decadent resort areas of southern Bali: it's spacious, quiet and there are usually more locals at the beaches and clubs than foreign tourists because of its proximity to Mataram, the capital. Spend the morning exploring the streets and beaches of central Senggigi on foot, and then nosing about the **Art Market** (see page 88) before choosing one of the classy seaside cafés nearby for lunch, such as De Quake. Later, flag down a *bemo* (pick-up truck) or taxi and visit **Pura Batu Bolong temple** to the south. Then head north and walk (1.2km/0.75 miles) from the main road to the Taman Wisata Alam Kerandangan **nature reserve**. Finish the day with a sunset cocktail and dinner at **Café Alberto** (see page 84). For more information about Senggigi, refer to the special section on page 28.

Day 3: **Mataram**
The provincial capital shines

Only a few kilometers from Senggigi, Mataram is an Indonesian anomaly: a likable city with enough sights to justify at least one day of exploration. It extends about 8km (5 miles) from the colonial port of **Ampenan** to **Bertais**, home to a massive **produce market** and the Sweta (Mandalika) bus terminal, which has connections all over Lombok. Driving yourself around any Indonesian city is not for the faint-hearted, so take a taxi or charter a car with a driver. Start at 8am to fit in as many sights as possible.

The **Museum Negeri** (8am–4pm Sat–Thurs; 8–11.30am Fri) boasts a better-than-average assortment of geological, historical, and cultural

Pura Meru, Mataram

artefacts about the region and its people. The **Pura Mayura** water palace (daylight hours, daily) is a 350-year-old former court and temple which features a *bale kambang* pavilion in a pond connected by a walkway. Opposite, **Pura Meru** (daylight hours, daily) is Lombok's largest temple. Built almost 300 years ago, it features three courtyards, 30 shrines, and immaculate gardens, and is regularly used for elaborate ceremonies. The dual-religious **Pura Lingsar** temple is detailed in a special section (see page 27).

A little further east, the village of Suranadi is home to the oldest and most sacred Hindu temple on Lombok, the 16th century **Pura Suranadi** (7am–6pm daily). Locals also visit for the bathing **pools** in the adjacent hotel, which has an agreeable poolside café for lunch. Just down the road is the **Hutan Wisata Suranadi forest** (7am–6pm daily) with plenty of scenery, birdlife and, of course, monkeys to admire along some short trails. Spend the rest of the afternoon relaxing at the **Taman Narmada** park with its "Mini-Rinjani" (see page 29). Then return to Senggigi in time for pre-dinner drinks at the elegant **Taman Restaurant** (see page 84).

EXPLORING NORTHERN LOMBOK
Get up close and personal with Mount Rinjani, Lombok's mighty volcano

See Lombok inset on the folded map

You've probably been, or are going to, the pearls of Lombok's crown: the incomparable trio of islands known as the Gilis, the laidback resorts of Senggigi, and the hypnotic beaches of Kuta. But to experience the real Lombok away from the crowds and the heat, head into the hills, particularly The Big One.

Day 1: Road to Senaru
Endless beaches and coconut groves

Senggigi is the obvious starting point and the only place to reliably arrange transport. The trip to Senaru only takes 2–3 hours, but allow time to explore villages on the way, be in Senaru for lunch and wander about the nearby waterfalls in the afternoon (see Best Walks on page 115).

The coastline north of Senggigi is rugged and spectacular.

The resorts eventually run out north of Senggigi, but the spectacular beaches do not: one horseshoe bay after another lined with fishing huts, backed by coconut trees and interrupted by those elevated promontories that'll make your driver curse as you demand to stop for another photo. The Gili Islands appear at the twin harbors of **Teluk Kodek** and **Teluk Nara** (both used by speedboats from Bali) which are just before **Bangsal**, the frenzied transport hub for public boats to/from the Gilis. (Refer to page 62 for some survival tips.) The windy, coastal road continues past the turn-off to **Sira**, an expansive area of white sands and calm waters perfect for **swimming** and **snorkeling**. The main road soon heads into rocky, arid countryside and passes black-sand shores dotted with poor villages, many of which still follow the Islamic sect of Wektu Telu. For a glimpse of traditional life, visit **Segenter**, where locals show tourists around their village for a small fee. South of **Bayan**, a center of Wektu Tulu with its distinctive thatched mosques, the landscape becomes immediately fertile as Rinjani looms large and **Batu Koq** village merges into **Senaru**.

Although the focal point for trekking (see above), Senaru is certainly worth visiting for other reasons (see page 26). A dozen basic but comfortable homestays line the main road, but it's best to stay at or near Pondok Senaru, because the village road is steep, the entrance to the waterfalls is nearby, and the restaurant offers the best views and most diverse menu.

Day 2: To Tetebatu
Along Lombok's only mountain road

If you're not trekking up the volcano, the docile villages clinging to the fertile

Trekking Up Gunung Rinjani

Formed during an explosion 14,000 years ago, Gunung Rinjani (3,726m/ 12,224ft) is dormant, but Gunung Baru ("New Mountain") at 2,351m (7,713ft) inside the crater has erupted several times, most recently in 1994 when van-sized boulders hurled down the valleys. The **Taman Nasional Gunung Rinjani** national park was established in 1997 and now covers 41,330 hectares.

While organizing **treks** at the departure point (e.g., Senaru) cuts out the middleman, and allows you to talk to your guide and check his equipment, arranging everything in Senggigi or the Gili Islands is definitively advantageous (but more expensive) because the cost will include direct, private transport to the starting and finishing points. Deal with a reputable company, such as John's Adventures (rinjanimaster.com) or Rinjani Trekking Club (anaklombok.com), and you'll know the necessary equipment is included, guides and porters will be experienced, and everything will run smoothly — except, possibly, the weather, which can be unpredictable at any time. Note: the park closes (and trekking is prohibited) when the rains start in December/January and won't reopen until March/April. But during the **rainy season**, "soft trekking" (i.e., day hikes) to Pos I or II from Senaru or Sembalun Lawang is possible with a guide.

The trail from Senaru starts at the 600-meter (656-yd) high **Rinjani Trek Center** (0370-641124; lombokrinjanitrek.org; open 24/7). This is where trekkers register and pay an entrance fee (Rp150,000), which should be included if you've pre-booked with a trekking company. There are three main routes: (1) 2 days/1 night in and out of Senaru, overnighting at the camp site (2,641m/8,664ft) at the **Danau Segara Anak** crater lake; (2) 3 days/2 nights, including the hot springs, starting in Senaru and finishing at Sembalun Lawang (or vice versa); and (3) the masochist 4- or 5-day expedition, including the summit and caves, starting in Senaru and finishing at Sembalun Lawang (or vice versa). If you don't fancy camping or climbing too high, you can **walk** without a guide (in the dry season) for 2–3 hours one-way from Senaru to the Pos II post (1,500m/4,900ft). In Sembalun Lawang, contact the **Rinjani Information Center** (0819-17807636; open 7am–5pm daily) about treks and guides. Because this village is already high (1,156m/3,792ft), the 2½ hour hike to the Pos I post is comparatively gentle.

Inside the crater of Gunung Rinjani

The village of Sembalun Lawang, with Mount Rinjani behind

Day 3: Around Tetebatu
Leave the car and use your walking shoes

This is a day for delving into the countryside, which you can do yourself on foot or by hiking with a guide; every employee of every guesthouse and café in Tetebatu is a guide or related to one (see Best Walks on page 115).

Tetebatu's major drawcard is the **Air Terjun Jeruk Manis waterfalls**, 1.5km (0.93 miles) from the HQ of the Taman Nasional Gunung Rinjani national park, which is 5.5km (3.4 miles) up the steep road from the village (past Green Orry homestay). An easier 5km (3.1 miles) walk from Tetebatu along another spectacular ridge leads to the **Taman Wisata Otak Kokoq** gardens, home to the undersized **Air Terjun Joben waterfalls** and an Olympic-sized **swimming pool**, popular with locals on weekends.

slopes of Rinjani are still worth visiting, although Tetebatu along the southern perimeter has the best facilities. Start this excursion after exploring Senaru a little more during the morning.

You'll have to detour back to **Bayan** before the road climbs ferociously to **Sembalun Lawang**. This alternate, but poorly-developed, trekking base is positioned in a gorgeous valley famous for vegetables that can't be grown elsewhere. The four guesthouses are the only sources of information about **hikes** to nearby waterfalls and hills, and visiting **weaving workshops**. The patchy road continues south across one of Indonesia's highest mountain passes and leads to the turn-off for Sapit, another delightful mountain village. Jaw-dropping **views of Rinjani** can be admired over lunch at the Hati Suci Homestay.

From Sapit, take the well-worn route through Suwela, Aikmel, and Paokmotong to **Tetebatu**, set along a lush ridge with rice fields, waterfalls, and a trillion contented frogs. Along the main dead-end street and the road to the waterfalls are about 10 rustic homestays with restaurants. Tetebatu is the perfect place to try local **Sasak food**, particularly at Pondok Tetebatu or Green Orry.

Jeruk Manis waterfalls

EXPLORING SOUTHERN LOMBOK
Vast stretches of gorgeous
beachfront that are still
relatively undeveloped

*See Kuta (Lombok) inset on the folded
map*

The southern edges of Lombok are the
last vestiges of undeveloped beaches on
either island, but relocation of the international airport to within a 20-minute
taxi ride of Kuta will no doubt have enor-
mous consequences. But the terrible
roads east and west of Kuta will ensure
that much of the coast will remain free
of mega-resorts and hamburger joints
for a decade more at least. We hope.

Day 1: Praya to Kuta
Old villages with many changes afoot

Whether coming from Tetebatu or
Senggigi, you'll pass through
Praya, now the closest town to the airport. As traffic to Kuta becomes more
lucrative, a few art-and-craft shops now
line the road, but one authentic place to
stop and shop has always been **Penujak**
village. While still a major center for
Lombok's distinctive and decorative
style of clay pottery called *gerabah*,
the airport bypass road has seriously
affected business.

Also sprouting up along the road are
"traditional Sasak villages." The best is
still **Sade**, with its distinctive *lumbung*
rice barns with roofs of *alang-alang*
grass and floors of, um, cow dung (com-
pacted and dried). Tourists are welcome
to wander about, take photos, buy a souvenir, of course, and hire a guide for a
more enlightening experience. Other
Sasak villages nearby are more authentic and free to explore, such as **Penyalu**
on a hilltop behind Sade, while a few
hundred meters further towards Kuta
are some distinctive **longhouses**,
similar to those found on Borneo but for
storage not housing.

In this modern age of mass tourism,
it's almost inconceivable that somewhere
like **Kuta** could remain so untouched for
so long. But with flash offices and neon

Kuta Beach, Lombok

Laidback Kuta, Lombok

signs featuring words like "sales," "development," and "consultancy," dramatic changes are imminent. Beachside bamboo huts offering "loundry" will soon be replaced with mini-marts, so this Kuta may quickly (and, probably, hastily) resemble the other one in Bali. Contemplate this while spending the afternoon enjoying Kuta's laidback charms around the streets and beaches, and later enjoying dinner at a beachside café such as **Solah** (see page 84). For more information about the current version of Kuta, refer to page 25.

Day 2: Southwest Coast
Rugged, remote, and restless

After exploring the streets and beaches of Kuta during the morning, buckle up and rodeo-ride this collection of rocks and potholes termed a "road." After two kilometers, you'll want to stop for lunch at **Astari**, a classy hilltop restaurant (closed Monday) which features a diverse menu and gorgeous panoramas. From **Bangkang** views of the astonishing bays you're about to discover will encourage you to endure the road a little further to **Mawun**, a pristine and almost circular bay with undertows dangerous for swimming. Astoundingly, the remainder of the road is fine. **Selong Blanak** is another magnificent protected cove with sunset views and a

friendly fishing village. The road continues inland and heads to **Lembar**, the harbor for ferries to Bali and boats to sparsely-developed islands nearby, such as **Gili Nanggu**. To avoid that despicable road again, head north to Penujak and take the main road south back to Kuta. Then, perhaps, finish the day at **The Shore Beach Bar** (see page 92).

Day 3: Southeast Coast
Heavenly beaches and decent roads

In contrast, the road along the southeast coast is acceptable. The perfect U-shaped bays of golden sands are no doubt already earmarked on blueprints in offices of development companies in Seoul and Jakarta. The first stop (3.6km/ 2.23 miles)—but half the distance along the beach (with a detour around one hill)—is a gorgeous, sheltered bay with rocky islets called **Pantai Seger**, where there are usually more goats than tourists. You think you've found heaven, but wait... Just 2.4km (1.5 miles) further on is **Pantai Aan**, where the sand is even whiter, the sea bluer, and the bay almost circular. It's also the finest spot for **swimming** and **snorkeling** anywhere around Kuta. Have lunch at one of the two beachside **cafés** along the western end and try to remember if you've ever seen a beach so perfect. This road ends after another 1.5km (0.93 miles) at **Gerupuk**, a thriving village that produces seaweed and lobsters and has a lucrative sideline in homestays, shops, and boats for weather-beaten surfers. Another option is to head back towards Kuta and take a short cut to the excellent bypass road that leads to the fishing village of **Awang**, with its abandoned port and mangrove bays.

CHAPTER 3
AUTHOR'S RECOMMENDATIONS

You'll need to make frequent and often rapid decisions not only about places to stay and eat, but where and how to spend your precious time and money in the malls, clubs, spas, and beaches. And don't forget the kids also want to have a real, like, "rad time," dude. The choices in Bali and, to a lesser extent, Lombok are truly extraordinary, so we've relieved you of some the decision-making "stress" by listing the author's personal recommendations of the very best of the best, based on extensive research and his knowledge and experience from traveling and working throughout both islands. Also included are brief guides to the tastiest local cuisine and most worthwhile souvenirs.

BEST HOTELS ON BALI & LOMBOK

From family-run inns to luxury villas and resorts

Finding a room is rarely a problem, except during the peak seasons of mid-December to late January (main Australian school holidays) and July and August (when Europeans flock). There are a few other things to bear in mind, too. Budget places (often called homestays) in tourist areas will only have a fan and cold water, and you provide toilet paper, towel, and, often, top sheet if needed. (Other linen is provided.) A medium-priced room will include air-conditioning, hot water (but not always) and, probably, breakfast. Wi-Fi is common in all categories, although often only accessible around the reception and restaurant. A popular alternative to hotels are furnished villas or bungalows which usually come with a kitchen, living room, and several bedrooms, maybe even a pool. These can be rented by the day or week, but most commonly by the month or even year. Check out the bulletin boards in Ubud (e.g. at Bali Buddha Café and Bintang Supermarket), in local newspapers (see page 120), and websites such as balivillas.com.

SOUTHERN BALI

Suji Bungalows, Kuta (budget)
The unassuming entrance from the road opens out to a welcome expanse of palm trees and flourishing lawns. A large selection of accommodation is on offer, from the cheap and cheerful motel-style rooms at the back with fan and private balcony to cottages and detached bungalows with all the mod cons. Worth booking ahead is a two-story bungalow shaped like a *lumbung* (traditional rice barn) with a double-bed upstairs and spacious lounge area with two extra beds downstairs. The pool with its slide for the kids and bar for the adults is very inviting, as are the swinging seats dotted around the lawn. For many, the attractions are the space, peace, and privacy (words not usually synonymous with Kuta) and the opportunity to enjoy three-star facilities at a one-star price.
Gang Sorga, off Poppies Lane 1; 0360-765804; sujibglw.com

Three Brothers Bungalows, Legian (budget to medium)
One of the oldest is still one of the very best. With space and lawns the envy of five-star resorts elsewhere, the site is deceptively large and almost unique in that most of the area is lawn rather than buildings. Rooms range from the simple with fan and cold water to two-storey deluxe villas with all the frills, including sparkling tiled bathrooms larger than most hotel rooms. The delightful gardens are designed so that the foliage provides welcome privacy, and unlike so many hotels of this vintage it doesn't feel or look dated. The attractive restaurant opens out to the main road and overlooks a large swimming pool surrounded with palm trees, while most rooms (and the reception) are some 200m (218yds) further away. Frequent renovations (e.g. open-plan bathrooms), thoughtful design (e.g. private balco-

nies), and acceptable rates ensure that the Three Brothers remains extremely popular.
Jalan Padma Utara; 0361-751566; threebrothersbungalows.com

Raja Gardens Bungalows, Seminyak (medium)

Located under the gaze of the elegant St Mikael's Church, this delightfully understated hotel is set along a quiet street only a one-minute walk from the main drag. It offers a small number of rooms, each almost swallowed by foliage, and surrounded by an immaculate lawn. Run by a congenial family who live on site (a rarity in this area), the hotel is under-promoted and easy to miss, so it's rarely fully occupied, which suits the handful of long-staying guests (who'll be annoyed that it's recommended in this guidebook). The enticing pool is larger than you'd expect and you'll probably have it to yourself, although you'll be sharing the gardens with the numerous birds, frogs, and geckos. The deluxe rooms have been lovingly renovated with four-poster beds, charming open-air bathrooms and commodious lounge chairs on private balconies.
Jalan Abimanyu; 0361-730494; sites.google.com/site/rajagardens

W Retreat & Spa, Petitinget (luxury)

This extraordinary new resort seems obsessed with the 23rd letter of the alphabet, evidenced by the Wired & Word business center and Woo Bar, so in keeping with their passion for alliteration... It's Wide—guests are issued a two-page map of the grounds which are the size of a village and offered buggy rides to the main road. It's Welcoming—with immaculately-trained staff, and touches like a "Good Morning" rug in the lifts (changed every afternoon and evening). It's Wonderful—the 237 rooms, suites and villas have facilities like an automated skylight in the bathroom and wall-mounted TV hidden behind a sliding mirror. And it's Wow—with cascading swimming pools facing the sea and enough spas, gyms and shops to ensure that you'll never need that buggy.
Jalan Petitenget; 0361-4738106; whotels.com/baliseminyak

W Retreat & Spa, Petitinget

Sativa Sanur Cottages, Sanur (medium)

Tucked away in a quiet corner of southern Sanur, this compact group of bungalows is a rare example where Balinese elegance, style, and charm mean much more to the owners than whiz-bang gadgets and needless concrete. It's refined and elegant, with dragons spouting water into the elongated and curved pool, complete with islets of coconut palms; the large overhanging roofs are thatched; and a raised reception deck overlooks the dense foliage. The sizable rooms contain sofas and other four-star facilities (at a two-star price), and the wide balconies face the pool. And there would be views of the beach (only 200m/ 218yds away) from the back windows if there wasn't another abandoned and unfinished resort in the way.
Jalan Cemara; 0361-287881; sativahotels.com

Tandjung Sari, Sanur (luxury)

So many hotels try to incorporate a "Balinese" design and style, but most fail as they install bright lights and fancy swimming pools, and squeeze too many rooms into a confined space. By contrast, Tandjung Sari was built way back in 1962 with a purpose and design that encapsulates the traditional village spirit (though all mod cons are included). Among the spacious gardens, which are dotted with traditional sculptures and fish ponds, are secluded bungalows of various shapes, sizes, and frontage, all elegantly, but not ostentatiously, furnished with four-poster beds and sunken baths. And the "Flower Cape" hotel offers other charming touches, like Balinese-style *bale* pavilions for relaxing, and a convivial library.
Jalan Danau Tamblingan 41; 0361-288441; tandjungsarihotel.com

The Laguna Resort & Spa, Nusa Dua

The Laguna Resort & Spa, Nusa Dua (luxury)

Every multi-star resort in the gated complex of Nusa Dua has lobbies with *gamelan*-players and chandeliers the size of spaceships; all have luxurious rooms with mod cons you probably didn't realize you needed; and each has villas best accessed by golf buggy. And they all have enough shops, bars, and restaurants to ensure that you never have to leave the front gate, which could be 500m (546yds) away. But what makes The Laguna really special are the extra facilities and superb location. There are a dozen swimming pools the shape of lagoons (hence the name) — some with waterfalls, fountains and, yes, even small beaches — and plenty of activities for the kids and anyone else who wants to get off their loungers. And it is one of the few resorts that has beach frontage and is within walking distance of the Bali Collection mall, where all the independent shops, bars, and restaurants in Nusa Dua are (in)conveniently located.
0361-771327; thelagunabali.com

Rumah Bali, Tanjung Benoa (medium to luxury)

It's difficult, if not impossible, to find any medium-priced accommodation in

this neck of the woods, and when it's somewhere as exceptional as this it's time to get excited. Part of the fabulously successful Bumbu Bali company that runs restaurants and cooking courses, Rumah Bali is designed like a Balinese village (albeit with a swimming pool and tennis court) and set on an immense block with striking foliage and manicured lawns dotted with contemplative *bale* pavilions. Yet the entrance is only 100m (109yds) from the main road and 200m (218yds) from the beach. A wide range of accommodation is on offer, but the villas with private plunge pools, kitchens, and dining areas naturally cost three or four times more than the cheapest rooms. All the accommodation is beautifully decorated with stunning bathrooms, and fenced off to provide peace and privacy.
Jalan Pratama; 0361-771256;
bedandbreakfastbali.com

Four Seasons, Jimbaran (luxury)

Spread along both sides of a lengthy, steep road in southern Jimbaran, the Four Seasons has arguably the widest and most diverse views anywhere on Bukit Peninsula, where you'll see golden sands turn tangerine at sunset and then the twinkling of candle-lit beachside restaurants after dark. The resort is large enough to offer — and need — golf buggies, because some villas and the associated Jimbaran Beach Club are at sea level, while the rest of the 150 villas cascade up the hill surrounded by a forest of frangipani trees. The villas are truly opulent with private pools and jaw-dropping views. You can dine at the cliff-top restaurant or stroll (or buggy) down to the seafood cafés along the beach. The resort even has its own art showroom — the **Ganesha Gallery** (see page 101). And unlike so many other villa complexes across the Bukit Peninsula, the Four Seasons boasts its own expansive private beach and is in walking distance of shops and cafés.
Jalan Pantai Jimbaran; 0361-701010;
fourseasons.com/jimbaranbay

Anantara Bali Uluwatu Resort & Spa, Padang-Padang (luxury)

The southern edge of Bukit Peninsula is dotted with cliff-top villa resorts that are secluded (if you don't mind sharing with guests from the other 50 villas) but also remote; maybe 3km (1.86 miles) to the nearest shop. And, remarkably, very few have access to any beach at all. The sparkling new Anantara, however, is within walking distance of the adorable Padang-Padang beach and its cluster of bars, cafés, and shops. The 74 villas and suites (almost all with sea views) are spread across two hectares, with the serenity only interrupted by the sound of waves crashing against the cliffs 80m (260ft) below. The architecture is minimalist but elegant, and all the accommodation contains the expected luxuries including marble floors. The top-notch villas feature balcony spas, as well as plunge pools if you don't want to use the infinity-style horizon-level pool with other guests.
Jalan Pemutih, Labuan Sait;
0361-8957555;
wwwbali-uluwatu.anantara.com

UBUD

Nick's Pension (budget to medium)

This understandably longterm favorite extends from a jungle-clad ravine (accessible down some steps and across a bridge from Jalan Monkey Forest road) all the way to those sublime rice fields

The Komaneka chain has four hotels in the Ubud area, including this one at Tanggayuda.

facing Jalan Bisma. The bungalows with private gardens and balconies are spacious, immaculate, and spread out, and the whole place just oozes a sense of tranquillity. Accommodation ranges from the simple with fan and cold water to the luxurious with most of the frills, and all boast the sort of views and location the five-star hotels would charge the earth for. The area facing the ravine is built up these days, however, as other homestays squeeze in and share the view, so the cottages at the back near the pool and restaurant are more appealing.
Jalan Bisma (also accessible from Jalan Monkey Forest); 0361-975636; nickshotels-ubud.com

Alam Indah (medium)
In a town full of delightful bungalows with rice field views, it seems harsh to recommend just one, but the Alam Indah ("Beautiful Nature") certainly ticks all the right boxes. Part of a small chain of similar bungalow complexes in Ubud, it's superbly positioned about 200m (218yds) down a road that skirts the Monkey Forest Sanctuary and leads to an undeveloped ravine. The bungalows are crafted from a delicious combination of thatch, rattan, and bamboo — all lovingly decorated.

The gardens are lush and pool is sublime, and staff offer extras like traditional cooking classes and walks among the *padi* fields. The management is proud and confident enough to advise guests that rooms do not feature "distractions" like televisions and telephones, so you'll just have to relax on the extensive balcony and listen to the orchestra of birds, geckos, and frogs.
Jalan Nyuh Bojog, Nyuhkuning; 0361-974629; alamindahbali.com

Komaneka at Bisma (luxury)
Luxury without isolation, seclusion without inconvenience, and a setting for which the resorts in Sayan further away in Ubud would charge considerably more… Layered down a ravine over four levels (complete with elevator), the Komaneka is super-sumptuousness, but somehow everything blends majestically into the environment. All the rooms and restaurants (even the gym) share the same views of the *padi* fields and distant volcanoes, are elegantly furnished, and feature ceiling-to-floor windows leading to broad balconies. All the mod cons are included, of course, but who wants to watch TV when the rates include tours of museums and lessons in arts & crafts, or you can luxuriate in one of those

elongated swimming pools that never seem to end? And all of this within a 15-minute walk of Monkey Forest Road.
Jalan Bisma; 0361-976090; komaneka.com

EASTERN BALI

Ida Beach Village, Candidasa (medium)

One of Bali's more unique hotels is designed like a traditional village and tucked away at the quiet, southeastern end of Candidasa, 400m (437yds) from the busy road. The bright, airy cottages with thatched roofs are separated by walls, surrounded by private gardens and individually named after local villages. The furniture is sparse but functional, with comfortable rattan chairs and polished tiled bathrooms. The two-story bungalows shaped like a *lumbung* (traditional rice barn) are more rustic, but the ground-floor lounge area is inviting and they do boast sea views. Opened more than 20 years ago, the Ida Beach is still lovingly maintained, with a pool, rare pocket of private beach, and breakwater providing a protected swimming area in the sea.
Jalan Pantai Indah; 0363-41118

Tirta Ayu Hotel, Tirtagangga (luxury)

This is your chance to live like a king or queen and imagine what it was like to rule this part of Bali. Well… almost. Tucked inside the enchanting Tirtagangga water palace, this unique hotel offers a handful of elegantly-furnished and lovingly-designed rooms with four-poster beds and sunken baths, all surrounded by dense foliage. The balconies don't have views of the gardens, but the whole complex of fountains, lawns, and ponds are at your doorstep and easy to explore after the tour groups have left.

The deluxe villa includes facilities fit for a king, with throne-like chairs and a private plunge pool, while the service offered to all guests is suitably regal. This may be one place to splurge on something unique. Look for special rates on their website and online booking agencies.
Tirtagangga water palace; 0363-22503; hoteltirtagangga.com

CENTRAL HIGHLANDS & NORTH COAST

Rambutan Beach Cottages, Lovina (budget to medium)

This oldie but goldie is deceptively spread out across a hectare of lush gardens in Kalibukbuk with not one requisite pool (the beach is so unappealing) but two — and both are so shady and inviting that you may never leave your deckchair. The rooms are pleasantly furnished and offer some genuine peace and privacy, while the villas are surprisingly large and luxurious, with four-poster beds and garden-style bathrooms. Consider this place if you're on a budget because guests in the cheaper fan-fuelled rooms eat the same breakfast, use the same pools and enjoy the same facilities as those in the villas. The playground, ping-pong table, and badminton court are further reasons why families also enjoy staying at "The Hairy Thing" (the literal translation of the fruit "rambutan").
Jalan Mawar; 0362-41388; rambutan.org

GILI ISLANDS & WESTERN LOMBOK

Alam Gili, Gili Trawangan (medium)

What you're probably craving is privacy, solitude and virtual beach frontage with-

in walking (but not hearing) distance of all the Bob Marley bars, and with most of the mod cons. Well, the Alam Gili offers it all—except unwanted distractions like televisions, telephones, and Wi-Fi (not available along this part of the island). Part of the excellent range of Alam hotels established in Ubud, this charming place provides a range of accommodation dotted around lush gardens along the slumberous northern coast, but still only 25 minutes' walk from the central strip of bars and cafés. The bungalows have ceiling fans and the villas have air-con, although the whole area is remarkably breezy, and the hotel boasts an inviting pool, although you're only meters from an immaculate and shady beach. Each room has the sort of lounge chair on the balcony that you'll want to curl up in and read, and the open-air bathrooms are a delight.
North coast; 0370-630466; alamindahbali.com/alam_gili.htm

Windy Beach Resort, Senggigi (medium)

Sometimes the original is still the best. The owners may have partially changed the name from "Cottages" to "Resort," but otherwise they refuse to upgrade or rebuild and become "villa-fied" like its trendy neighbors. The thatched cottages (which have still been renovated over the years) are well-furnished with wide balconies, are spread out among a coconut grove and face one of Senggigi's best beaches at Mangsit. Families are well-catered for with larger rooms, and everyone will appreciate the spacious lawns and inviting pool. And a good night's sleep is assured, which can *not* be said for The Nightclub Nightmare known as central Senggigi, which is

5km (3.1 miles) away and easily accessible by taxi or public transport.
Main road, Mangsit; 0370-693191; windybeach.com

NORTHERN LOMBOK & RINJANI

The Oberoi, Lombok (luxury)

There are few multi-star resorts on Lombok for comparison, but this sumptuous place would rate very highly anywhere in Bali or Southeast Asia. It's set among 24 hectares of luxuriant tropical gardens and backs on to that sublime beach you may've admired from the shoreline cafés of Gili Air. The award-winning villas are designed with traditional Sasak influences, such as thatched roofs, and feature indigenous wall-hangings and artefacts. You may never want to roll off that massive four-poster bed, except to hang around the type of swimming pool they feature in glossy magazines. The resort is expansive but intimate, and guests rave about the staff's attention to detail. And it's only a short ride to those sparkling Gili Islands across the strait. The Oberoi ticks every box imaginable, except that it's now further from the airport (which is 90 minutes south by taxi).
Medana beach; 0370-6138444; oberoihotels.com/oberoi_lombok

The Oberoi, Lombok

BEST FOOD & RESTAURANTS ON BALI & LOMBOK

Roast pig on a side-street or seafood on the beach

One of the primary attractions for many is the variety of food available in the vast number and array of restaurants featuring friendly staff and, often, superb locations and elegant decor. On either island, you can eat cheap, authentic food in a *warung* (food stall) or in an expensive, western-style bistro where you may have to book a day in advance. The choice is endless, but we've provided some recommendations, so *selamat makan* (bon appetit)!

SOUTHERN BALI

Poppies, Kuta
Opened way back in 1973, Poppies offers two rare commodities: space and privacy. The menu is concise (with a reasonable wine list), and it's an ideal place to try local cuisine such as *ikan pepes* (spicy fish in banana leaves), perhaps followed by its famous mango cheesecake. With pebbles underfoot and vine leaves atop, Poppies is elegant but unfussed, with prices that would triple if in Seminyak.
Poppies Lane 1; 0361-751059; poppiesbali.com

Waroeng Tan Poh, Kuta
This gem is tucked away along a quiet, village-style street less than 100m

(109yds) from the maniacal traffic. It offers friendly staff and a charming setting with fountains and plenty of shade "under the manggoes tree" (according to the signs). The menu (with helpful photos) is comprehensive and thoughtful, so there are no jaffles or pancakes. Sit down, take a deep breath, and enjoy your meal before heading back into that Kuta chaos.
Lane between Jalan Legian and Jalan Lebek Bene

Lanai Beach Bar & Grill, Legian
Among a cluster of beachside eateries where Legian merges into Seminyak, this place features an extensive, shady upper floor with uninterrupted views at sunset and breezes at other times. The variety is impressive: perhaps try Vietnamese rolls for entree, fettuccine seafood for main course, and *pisang goreng* (fried bananas) for desert? And the Lanai is also perennially popular for its cocktails and monster breakfasts.
Beach promenade, just south of Jalan Arjuna (Double Six); 0361-731305

Warung Murah, Legian
As an antithesis to the concrete and pretense nearby, this *warung murah* (cheap food stall) is popular with Indonesians (always a good sign). The setting is basic, with wooden chairs and fans, but the staff are very congenial. There's a menu, but most choose their own *nasi campur*—steamed rice with a choice of 15 or more extras, such as fish curry and beef *rendang*, all heated and hidden from the dust outside.
Jalan Double Six 99; 0361-732082

Chez Gado Gado, Seminyak
This classy place overlooking the beach offers a menu and wine list that's both extensive and expensive. While unasham-

Chez Gado Gado, Seminyak

edly French-influenced, the menu has splashes of Greek, Thai, and Balinese, while the seafood — such as the grilled kingfish — is understandably popular. At lunch, tablecloths are removed and a cheaper menu is offered, so dishes like *babi guling* (roast pig) are excellent value. *Jalan Dhyana Pura (Camplung Tandak); 0361-736966; gadogadorestaurant.com*

Made's Warung, Seminyak

The modest entrance belies a huge eating area circled by classy shops (including a Periplus bookshop). Most evenings from about 6.30pm patrons can enjoy (for no extra charge) a variety of genuine traditional dances on the large stage while woofing down any number of western and Balinese dishes, as well as the popular set-priced three-course menu of Indonesian food. Bookings are recommended.
Jalan Raya Seminyak; 0361-732130; madeswarung.com

La Lucciola, Petitenget

What a magnificent setting: an open-air, thatched pavilion fronting an immaculate lawn with sloping coconut palms only meters from the crashing waves. Elegant without being pretentious, formal without being too sophisticated, La

Lucciola has a menu influenced by the Italian chef, but there's much more than just pasta, e.g., grilled seafood with Balinese spices. The lunchtime menu with daily specials is more affordable, but get there early for the sunset.
End of Jalan Petitenget; 0361-790838

Art Café Warung, Sanur

Along the stretches of "villa-fied" southern Sanur, this hangout has paintings for sale and magazines to read, and is popular with expats and tourists in the know who often arrive by bicycle. With seating indoors and out, the attraction is as much about the quiet, breezy vibe as the meals. And there are two bonuses: the chance to try the *rijstaffel* (Balinese buffet for two) and extensive wine list.
Jalan Mertasari 26; 0361-286366; balisekala.com

Sanur Beach Market Bar & Restaurant, Sanur

One of the most charming places along the promenade is owned by the Sanur Village Foundation, which helps build and maintain local schools, temples, and art centers. And you can tell the difference: the staff smile longer, the children happily perform the *Legong* dance (some nights) and the cooks grill your fish on the outdoor barbecue with gusto. Go on, order another Bintang. It's for a good cause. Free transport is available around Sanur.
Beachfront, closest to Jalan Segara Ayu; 0361-289374; sanurbeachmarket.com

Kendi Kuning, Nusa Dua

Straddling the invisible border between Tanjung Benoa and Nusa Dua, this lovely place is set under a canopy of shady trees, with tables spread across the immaculately raked (and even graded) sand. You can choose fresh seafood from the ice box

and watch it being grilled on the barbecue, or order from the extensive menu
(and wine list). With attentive service,
romantic setting, and muted background
music, this is understandably popular
with guests from both resort areas.
End of Jalan Segara; 0361-775720;
kendikuning.com

Paon Beach Club, Tanjung Benoa
Behind an ugly brick façade is the delightful Paon Beach Club, where you can
enjoy a drink on a sofa, rocking chair or
cushion, or around the pool, overlooking
the beach or on the lawn. The restaurant
in the open-air pavilion offers western
food and Indonesian delights such as the
tasty *dadar gulung* (coconut crepes). The
beach is scruffy (and quiet, with nary a
banana-boat in sight), but with such an
enticing pool, who really cares? It's also
perfect for kids.
Taman Bhagawan, Jalan Pratama 70;
0361-776555; paonbeachclub.com

Melasti Tanah Lot, Tanah Lot
On a headland just north of the majestic
temple, this place boasts one of the most
extraordinary settings in Bali. Under can-
dlelight, dig into succulent prawns, lobster,
or other fresh seafood while admiring the
world-famous sunset or after the *Kecak*
dance nearby. The menu is a la carte, but
the (expensive) set-priced meals do include some beer or wine. It's more affordable at lunch, but the prime cliff-side tables
are reserved for evening diners only.
Tanah Lot temple complex; 0361-7805024

UBUD
Ibu Oka
Still regarded as the only place for *babi
guling* (roast pig), the original Ibu Oka
restaurant was being demolished at the

time of research. So, head 200m
(218yds) up the road (following the
signs) to its sister eatery, which provides
more seats and better views, but the
same menu: pork, pork, or pork. Most try
the *spesial* (with rice, spicy sausage, skin
and vegetables) or *complit* (also with
soup). Order and then, um, pig out.
Jalan Suweta; 0361-976345

Bali Buddha
Located down "yoga street," this adorable spot proves that healthy can also be
delicious, and with almost everything
vegetarian and organic you can tell the
difference with the omelettes and fruit
salads. The shop below sells pastries and
quite possibly the mightiest muffins on
the planet. Bali Buddha is very relaxing,
with convivial cushions conducive to
chatting with strangers, but be warned:
what they regard as "distractions" (beer
and Wi-Fi) are deliberately *not* available.
Jalan Jembawan 1; 0361-978963;
balibuddha.biz

Murni's Warung
This four-story restaurant clinging to a
ravine has expanded since it was a *warung* (food stall) in 1974. From the entrance, steps lead down to another
eating area with even better views and a
classy lounge bar. The extensive menu
includes western favorites, as well as
frogs' legs and Thai curries, but the
selection of Indonesian and Balinese
dishes could be more imaginative. The
immaculate service, breezy setting, and
delicious cakes make Murni's a must.
Jalan Raya Ubud; 0361-975233;
murnis.com

Warung Biah Biah
How refreshing that somewhere cater-
ing for westerners doesn't offer anything

Warung Biah Biah

with French fries; in fact, it serves nothing but Balinese and Indonesian food. The menu features about 30 treats, mostly served in pockets of palm leaves "stapled" with thin strands of wood; you'll need four to five of them to fill you up. Guests are encouraged to use their hands, although cutlery is provided. Perhaps finish with a Barong Cookie flavored with coffee, rice or salt.
Jalan Goutama 1; 0361-978249

EASTERN BALI

Sails, Bunutan (Amed)

This elegant, breezy place has those fishing-village views you keep stopping to photograph. The décor has a nautical theme that matches the name, while staff pride themselves on the hygiene of their cooking and quality of ingredients. The menu features unusual western dishes like bangers and mash, as well as *mahi-mahi* fish in banana leaves, all at pleasingly acceptable prices. Another attraction is that the only passable beach in Amed is just 200m (218yds) down the road. Free local pick-up.
Main road; 0363-22006;
sailsrestaurantbali.com

CENTRAL HIGHLANDS & NORTH COAST

Bedugul Restaurant, Bedugul

At the southern end of Lake Bratan, Bedugul is a recreation area set up for, and used almost exclusively by, Indonesians, but inexplicably ignored by foreigners. After whirling around the lake on a speedboat, settle down for lunch at the best lakeside restaurant in Bali. Western food isn't offered, but you'd be crazy not to try the fresh *gurami* (grouper fish) or *udang* (prawns) with various sauces while watching the free entertainment: Indonesian families having so much fun.
Taman Rekreasi Bedugul; 0368-21197

Lesehan Ikan Bakar, Lovina

This simple eatery along the western edge of Lovina offers enjoyable seafood, sea views, and sea breezes. It's also *lesehan*, which involves squatting in a gazebo-style hut perched above the sand. (If you prefer sitting down with your shoes on, there are normal tables.) The *menu du jour* is *ikan bakar* (grilled fish) or prawns served with rice and vegetables—and priced for Indonesian tourists. It's only 1.8km (1.2 miles) by *bemo* or bicycle, or on foot along the beach from the traffic light at Kalibukbuk.
Jalan Raya Seririt; 0362-41223

NUSA LEMBONGAN

The Beach Club at Sandy Bay, Sunset Beach

Sunset Beach is gorgeous to look at but terrifying to swim in, so safely admire it from the deckchairs by the inviting pool. The list of wine and cocktails is longer than the food menu, probably because many simply plump for lobster, prawn, snapper, or tuna, grilled to perfection each evening using charcoaled coconut husks. But it's not all seafood: they claim their steaks come from "very happy cows." Open from 8am, free return transport is provided (minimum of two). *0828-97005656; sandybaylembongan.com*

GILI ISLANDS & WESTERN LOMBOK

Café Gili Triwangan, Gili Trawangan

This agreeable café straddling both sides of the main "road" has those "I-never-want-to-leave" cushions only meters from the sea, as well as more functional tables on the sand. It offers an appealing range of food and drinks, including grilled seafood, mega-kebabs, and a salad bar. The background music is sophisticated, but may morph into Marley after the sun has set (on the other side of the island). This place epitomizes the largest of the Gilis to a T. *East coast; 0878-64013096*

Gita Gili Restaurant, Gili Air

Lie back on a cushion and dream about building your own café or villa along the golden shoreline facing you. Then pick up the menu, decipher the Indo-glish (choose the "spring rool" with "sweat sauce for deep" at your peril) and enjoy grilled seafood or treats like salmon baguettes. If you're not venturing to Lombok, this is a perfect chance to try local Sasak food, such as *olah-olah* (vegetables in coconut sauce) which is delicious and spelt perfectly. *East coast; 0878-65484690*

Café Alberto, Senggigi

Alberto's enjoys a perfect position next to the upswing of the coastal road. With tables and lounge chairs on the immaculate sand, the menu is Italian-influenced with home-made pasta, as well as grilled steak and fish. Maybe combine a visit with a beach stroll or sunset views at the Pura Batu Bolong temple nearby. Then enjoy some cocktails, finish off with a "Vanilla with Whisky" for dessert, and take them up on their offer of free transport back. *Jalan Raya Batu Bolong; 0370-693039; cafealbertolombok.com*

The Taman Restaurant, Senggigi

It's almost impossible to fault this elegant café. The setting is superb, with ground-level garden seating and a thatched mezzanine level lined with art for sale. The menu has a tempting multi-national flavor, with nachos, spring rolls, *biryani*, and pasta, as well as local specialties like *ayam taliwang* (spicy chicken). The bakery and all-you-can-stuff-down-your-throat breakfasts are also popular, but it's the exquisite service that entices many patrons to return. Free transport in the local area. *Jalan Raya Senggigi Km 8; 0370-693842*

SOUTHERN LOMBOK

Solah Beach Bar & Restaurant, Kuta

Whether it's the beachside setting with thatched umbrellas, the treats not seen anywhere on Lombok outside Gili Trawangan—like porridge (with oats, not rice), or the old-fashioned movie nights—Solah is justifiably popular. Salads, all-day brunches, and grilled seafood can be washed down with lassis, wines, or cocktails. Maybe start the morning with some yoga, followed by a yummy breakfast of yoghurt and muesli? *Jalan Pantai (beach street); 0858-57542690*

QUICK GUIDE TO LOCAL FOOD

Babi Guling

AYAM TALIWANG (Lombok)—half-chicken baked over coconut husks and smothered with a sauce of chilies, peanuts, and tomatoes. Best at a *warung* (food stall).

BABI GULING (Bali)—young pigs are stuffed with spices and roasted for hours on a skewer. Renowned across the Gianyar district, but best at specialty restaurants like Ibu Oka in Ubud (see page 82).

BEBEK BETUTU (Bali)—crispy (stringy) duck is covered with spices, wrapped in leaves, and baked in a traditional stove for 12 hours, so it often needs to be ordered in advance.

BUBUR INJIN/HITAM—common dessert for tourists and breakfast for locals, this black (*hitam*) rice pudding comes with grated coconut and sugar, and is served hot or cold.

CAP CAY (pronounced, and sometimes spelt, *chap chai*)—stir-fried vegetables, which can be enhanced with seafood or any meat or chicken. Eaten with rice.

GADO-GADO—popular meal with lentils, boiled eggs, and vegetables covered with peanut sauce. It varies in quality and tends to be better at nicer restaurants.

IKAN PEPES—fish (*ikan*) or other seafood is wrapped and steamed in (non-edible) banana leaves, allowing the spices and flavor of the leaf to seep through.

NASI CAMPUR—"mixed rice" with bits and pieces like *tempe* (soybean cake), boiled egg, chicken, and vegetables around a heap of steamed white rice.

NASI GORENG—"fried rice" is virtually the national dish of Indonesia. The "special," or *istimewa*, will include a fried egg on top and be served with tasty extras like crackers and satays.

PELECING (Lombok)—a fiery tomato and chili sauce made with water spinach (*kangkung*) that smothers fish (*ikan pelecing*) or chicken (*ayam pelecing*). Proceed with caution!

RUJAK—appetizing mix of fresh fruit and raw vegetables topped with a sauce that differs among regions of Indonesia, but usually includes peanuts and chilies.

SATE LILIT (Bali)—satay (*sate*) sticks of skewered chicken, meat, or fish roasted over coconut husks (which adds to the flavor).

SAYUR URAB—steamed vegetables (*sayur*) boiled in coconut milk and eaten with rice. A safe choice in the cheaper eateries.

RENDANG—slow-cooked curry with beef (sometimes chicken) boiled in coconut milk. Best in a decent restaurant where the meat will be better.

SOTO AYAM—popular among Indonesians, this is a tasty and filling soup of chicken (*ayam*), noodles, and potatoes, with *sambal* (chili paste) and rice on the side.

BEST SHOPPING ON BALI & LOMBOK

Change some more money and dust off those credit cards

There's no shortage of places to flog your credit card and unload those wads of *rupiah* thickening your money belt. To maximize your shopping time, we have listed the best districts, streets, and malls on Bali and Lombok to hone your bargaining skills, and suggested some places that produce the finest locally-made goods.

SOUTHERN BALI

Jalan Laksmana, Seminyak

First things first: this street is often labelled as Jalan Laksmana on maps, always signposted as Jalan Kayu Aya and known among locals as Jalan Oberoi. With a vast array of cafés to help you recover from "shopaholicism" and some actual footpaths (behold!), this street—whatever you call it—provides the best shopping in the region. Approaching from the chaotic Jalan Legian, several clothes stores and art galleries are clustered together before the turn-off to Jalan Dupradi, such as **Divine Diva Bali** (divinedivabali.com) at #1a, a popular salesroom and workshop offering handmade items (including for ladies of a fuller size). At **Tata Kayu** (0361-735072) at #10, wooden products are lovingly hand-carved, from dining tables to ornaments to put on your own table

back home. Further down, **Sea Gypsy** (0361-731769) at #48 sells elegant jewelry and pearls enticingly positioned on wooden slats; and the popular clothes gallery **Salim Why Not** (whynot-shop.com) at #29 is obvious from the miniature *becak* (rickshaw) outside. Keep going and you'll come across another branch of **Ulu Watu** (uluwatu.co.id) at #37, which specializes in exquisite handmade Balinese lace, and the eclectic collection of clothes and ornaments designed by the flamboyant resident, **Paul Ropp** (paulropp.com) at #39. And the perfect place to finish is **Seminyak Square**, with its excellent cafés, flea market, and Periplus bookshop.

Sanur to Ubud

If traveling between the southern beaches and Ubud in a taxi or chartered car, consider taking a detour and visiting some of Bali's finest handicraft villages. (Driving yourself is not recommended, however, because of the traffic and one-way streets.) Starting from the eastern side of Denpasar, via Sanur, is **Batubulan**, where the main road is lined with workshops offering intricate rock statues of Buddha and other icons you'd need a forklift to move. More portable stone carvings are available at shops where the road continues into **Singapadu**, directly opposite the entrance to the Bali Bird Park. Then detour back towards Gianyar and stop at **Celuk**, renowned for its gold and silverware, especially jewelry — although the more authentic workshops with cheaper prices are along Jalan Jagaraga, away from the main road. Next is **Sukawati**, home to the much-hyped but underwhelming **Pasar Seni Sukawati** art market, with the usual collection of sarongs and uninspiring framed paintings. Then there's **Mas**,

An arts & crafts shop in Nyuhkuning, Ubud.

famous for wood carvings, particularly masks and puppets, where you can also watch the artisans at work. And you know you're approaching Ubud when the roads are suddenly lined with arts and crafts shops.

Bali Collection, Nusa Dua

Only in the past few years has this mall improved to the point that it's now worth visiting more than once. It features the sort of shops you'd find in Kuta or Seminyak, but with shade and footpaths, and no traffic or hawkers, it makes shopping a real pleasure. With very few chain stores and international food/drink outlets, most of the shops and eateries are independent and interesting—not samey and repetitive. A map (available at the entrances) is vital, and shows the location of the **Sogo** department store and eight spas, as well as the 24 places to eat, which are conveniently bunched together so prices are competitive. There are souvenir stores the size of train stations, but also quaint **art galleries** and shops selling authentic Balinese goods such as **Meli-Meli** (for cushions and home furnishings), **T & L** (pearls), and **Rock Art** (designer T-shirts).
0361-771662; bali-collection.com; free shuttle bus around Nusa Dua and Tanjung Benoa, 10am–9pm

Traditional Markets, Denpasar

OK, you've strolled around the art markets and air-conditioned malls, so now it's time to experience shopping "Indonesian" style. You'll probably smell the **Pasar Badung** produce market (24 hours a day) as soon as you alight from the taxi. Set alongside a fetid canal, with a **temple** perched on an islet, this is a four-story conglomeration of captivating chaos. There are no trolleys, cash registers, or manners, everything is negotiable, and the slabs of unidentifiable meat hanging from hooks may put you off ordering another beef *rendang* for a while. Opposite, the **Pasar Kumbasari** art and clothing market (daily 9am–9pm) has lost some of its mojo as it fails to compete with the malls, but you can pick up sarongs and other souvenirs for a song. To complete your introduction to "Indonesian Marketing 101," walk 1km (0.62 miles) up Jalan Veteran to the **Pasar Burung** bird market (daily 9am–9pm). Animal lovers may want to break open the cages containing the dogs, cats, and rabbits, but the multitude of birds for showing, singing and, probably, stewing are fascinating.
Pasar Badung & Pasar Kumbasari (Jalan Gajah Mada); Pasar Badung (Jalan Veteran)

UBUD

Jalan Hanoman

Far more interesting and stylish than Monkey Forest Road, which is lined with tacky souvenir stalls and mini-marts, Jalan Hanoman is the main road through Pedangtegal village, so there are temples and even rice fields, as well as stylish cafés and boutiques selling elegant Balinese-made goods. Heading south from Jalan Raya Ubud, a few shops specializing in silver quickly emerge, with the best **Studio Perak** (studio-perak.com) also offering classes in jewelry-making. **Dari Bali** (0819-99315285) at #23 means "from Bali" and sells nothing but exquisite handbags and baskets made from rattan. **Truth** at #35 sells soaps and other natural skin-related products made from flowers, such as frangipani. The lucky number is #44, where all matters spiritual are catered for, including shops selling meditation books and yoga gear, such as **Bali Spirit**. Next door, **Tegun Folk Art Gallery** (tegungaleri.com) offers a wonderful variety of souvenirs, including puppets and masks, at remarkably attractive prices. The road soon changes its name to Jalan Pengosekan, and the best shopping really finishes at **Namaste** (0361-796178) at #64, with its alluring collection of incense and jewelry.

EASTERN BALI

Tenganan

It's hard to imagine a shopping experience more removed from the malls and markets of the southern beaches than this traditional village (see pages 47–48). Along cobblestoned paths, local men can show you how they make calendars, maps of Bali, and bookmarks using *lontar* palm leaves as *wayang kulit* puppets swing in the breeze waiting to be bought. Weaving is a major local industry, especially the intricate double-*ikat* style known as *geringsing* that's only found here. Unobtrusive stone doorways lead to large family compounds which serve as factories and showrooms where you can watch artisans at work. Not surprisingly, this is followed by a hard sell, but it's all good-natured. The "muzak" is the chickens clucking, you may have to

A textile seller in the traditional village of Tenganan

share the footpath with a cow and there's no shopping trolley or cash register for miles. Tenganan is more than a place to shop: it's a living, breathing mega-mall of genuine traditional village life.

GILI ISLANDS & WESTERN LOMBOK
Pasar Seni Art Market, Senggigi

You may've visited a few *pasar seni* (art markets) and been disappointed with the motley collection of stalls selling Bintang T-shirts, with the only "art" being those carved bottle-openers shaped like huge, um… Well, anyway, this one is unique: it's purpose-built (and not a white elephant), spacious (and not claustrophobic), and the stall-owners won't hassle you (too much). It is small and some stalls do sell "I Love Lombok" T-shirts — which, at least, makes a change from the Balinese version — but there's plenty that's unique to Lombok, including pearls, ceramic pottery, and *batik*-style handbags. The specialty stores (not stalls), such as **Treasure Chest Gift Shop**, **ABI Pearl Shop**, and **Karyana Fine Art Gallery** are inviting, and the market is only meters from a beach lined with classy cafés and bars.
Jalan Raya Senggigi Km 9

QUICK GUIDE TO HANDICRAFTS & ARTS ON BALI AND LOMBOK

CARVINGS: Roofs, gates, tables… *everything* in Bali seems to be elaborately carved. More portable wood-carvings are the *wayang kulit* shadow **puppets**, which are best in Tenganan and Nyuhkuning (Ubud), and **masks** at Mas along the road between Sanur and Ubud. Massive **stone statues** are available along the road through Batubulan, but more compact ones are at Singapadu nearby.

CLOTHES: The cloth called batik is made using dyes and decorated with colorful patterns using wax. The word *batik* also describes the bright **shirts** that are virtually the Indonesian national costume for men. The cotton wrap-around **sarong** is useful for ensuring modesty when swimming and for wearing at temples. Outfits worn by Balinese women during ceremonies, including *kebaya* blouses, are made from lace or cotton. Clothes and fabrics can bought from specialty stores (or from the head of a wandering market trader), but more authentic at the markets in Ubud and Denpasar.

JEWELRY: Popular gifts and souvenirs are bracelets, earrings, and necklaces made of **silver** or **gold** from specialty stores in Ubud, shops in and around the markets in Denpasar, and workshops around Celuk (on the road south of Ubud). **Pearls** harvested on special farms on Lombok and the neighboring island of Sumbawa are authentic and particularly good value at the **Art Market** in Senggigi.

PAINTING: For many centuries, Balinese art was mostly used to recount religious and historic tales and to decorate palaces and temples. Artistic creativity peaked in the 1930s when foreign interest, influence, and money brought Bali — and, in particular, Ubud — to the fore. Although now mostly mass-produced with limited creativity and imagination, paintings of landscapes and village life do make superb souvenirs. The best paintings are on display at Ubud, especially in the numerous museums and galleries (see pages 100–102).

WEAVING: The most elegant of Bali's three authentic styles of *ikat* cloth is *songket*, which is hand-woven from cotton or silk and features simple designs and bright colors using gold or silver threads. The other two styles are *endek*, which is best in Sidemen, and the double-*ikat geringsing* that's unique to Tenganan. Otherwise, all types of textiles are available in regional markets.

LOMBOK

One handicraft that Lombok excels in (and even surpasses Bali) is terracotta **pottery**. Bowls and vases with unpretentious designs but expert craftsmanship have been made for decorative and functional purposes since the 15th century in the specialist villages of Banyumulek and Penujak. **Baskets** from bamboo, palm leaves, and rattan grass are also popular.

An artist paints *wayang kulit* puppets at the Rudang Museum, Ubud.

BEST NIGHTSPOTS

After that great ball of fire has set, the party begins

Not surprisingly, most nightspots are where the tourists—and, more particularly, the younger ones—hang out, which means Kuta and Gili Trawangan, not Padangbai and Lovina. Few places have cover charges unless it's a particularly well-known act and only the really snooty places in Seminyak and Petitenget worry if you're wearing a singlet and sandals. And please take the usual precautions about spiked drinks and hanging about (especially inebriated) after closing. Everything you need is in the excellent, free bi-weekly gig guide *The Beat* (beatmag.com).

SOUTHERN BALI

M Bar Go, Kuta

The minimalist décor inside this pulsating palace is described by *The Beat* magazine as "sophisticated industrial urban." Indeed, the black interior doesn't look inviting, but after a bellyful of Bintangs nobody cares. The action is spread over two floors, with the usual cocktail specials, and resident and international DJs serving up the latest mix of hip-hop, dance, and house music to people who can tell the difference.
Jalan Legian 66; 0361-756280

SkyGarden, Kuta

Also called "61 Legian," this monstrous place actively seeks revelers all day long with offers like "free beer & bbq" and "girls drink for free." Hordes pack the floors until 2am every night in the eight—yes, *eight*—pubs and clubs, including the rooftop Sky Dome Super Club with international DJs and fire shows, and dance clubs with "go-go" dancers. There's even an Irish pub, *begorra.*
Jalan Legian 61; 0361-755423; skygardenbali.com

JP's Warung Club, Seminyak

If your head's still vibrating from last night's overdose of doof-doof music, head to this unassuming restaurant-club along a street far quieter than Jalan Legian. Different bands and solo musicians playing acoustic, jazz and rock perform every night from 9pm, and there's always something else interesting like seafood buffets and salsa nights to entice. You can enjoy the show from lounge chairs, tables in the decent restaurant, or convivial bar counter.
Jalan Dhyana Pura (Jalan Camplung Tanduk) 6; 0361-731622; jps-warungclub.com

Mannekepis, Seminyak

This delightfully relaxed and unpretentious restaurant offers live music three or four times a week, mostly jazz, soul, and piano. The extensive menu was designed by Balinese and Finnish chefs and features well-priced dishes like "Kill the Cook" (with imported Australian steak) and desserts called "Chocolate Orgasm." Otherwise, plonk yourself down for a drink at the inviting bar after enjoying dinner and a traditional dance at Made's Warung next door (see page 81).
Jalan Raya Seminyak 2; 0361-8475784; mannekepis-bistro.com

Hu'u, Petitenget

This unpronounceable spot is popular with well-heeled and high-heeled local pop stars and wannabes, as well as tourists and expats in the know. This modern, chic complex features a restaurant, bar and club, as well as a swimming pool fed by a spring, so you can eat, drink, and splash about before the music starts. There's a cover charge when renowned international DJs feature, but free when local artists—such as MC Gooze—appear.

Jalan Petitenget; 0361-4736576;
huubali.com

Jazz Bar & Grille, Sanur

One of a limited number of options in "S'nore" after the sun has set (in Kuta), this club features soul, R&B, and jazz performed by a variety of local, Indonesian, and foreign artists. The décor is sophisticated and intimate, with a ground level suited to watching and dancing, and a mezzanine level more conducive to chatting and listening. The restaurant (open from 10am) features an extensive menu with, as the name suggests, a focus on grilled meats and seafood. It's conveniently located on a major intersection (and next to Colonel Sanders' big head).

Jalan Raya Ngurah Rai 15-16; 0361-285892

UBUD

Café Havana

Salsa in Ubud? Latin grooves in the cultural heart of Bali? *Porque no*? It's a cocktail bar and *cantina* specializing in Latino cuisine, such as *tapas* and *paella*, where staff wear Che Guevera berets and salsa on the dance floor during quieter moments. The in-house band does their best Santana impressions every night

Jazz Bar & Grille, Sanur

(except Monday and Thursday) as bongo drums reverberate across the packed dance floor. It's so unusual, so un-Ubud and so damn irresistible. The old red Chevy usually parked out the front offers free lifts for guests.

Jalan Dewi Sita; 0361-972973
cafehavanabali.com

Jazz Club Tebesaya

Separate from, but related to, the Jazz Café in the Laughing Buddha on Monkey Forest Road, the one in Tebesaya village was the first of its kind in Bali. While the menu is intriguing and wine list is vast, most come for the entertainment (for which there's no cover charge). Every night (but Monday), you can dance, jive, boogie, or even sit and listen to soul, R&B, funk and, of course, jazz from the delightfully Ubudish time of 7.30 to 10.30pm. There's free pick up, and staff even provide free lessons in salsa, which you could later show off at the Café Havana.

Jalan Sukma 2; 0361-976594;
jazzcafebali.com

GILI ISLANDS & WESTERN LOMBOK

Rudy's Pub, Gili Trawangan

Like Kuta, the nightlife here is a main attraction, especially if it includes Magic

Mushrooms and half-price-cocktails-for-ladies nights. One long-standing ritual of any jaunt to Gili T is a session at Rudy's, followed by a hangover that no amount of swimming and sleeping will cure. Rudy's offers an impressive list of cocktails, especially designed to encourage you to belt out another chorus of "No Woman, No Cry" with the house band.
main street

Tir Na Nog, Gili Trawangan

While ostensibly an Irish pub with a Celtic name, there's an unusual lack of Guinness, shamrocks, and leprechauns. One of few places where Bob Marley CDs are not on perpetual rotation, this is a class way above Rudy's. There's the obligatory ultra-wide-screen TV and ultra-long bar counter, as well as a fancy restaurant facing the sea. And from 10pm DJs do their stuff and don't stop until the last guest is too inebriated to dance any more. A highlight is the weekly "Silent Disco" in which patrons dance with themselves wearing headphones. No, really.
0370-639463; tirnanogbar.com

Papaya Café, Senggigi

As no industrial-strength ear plugs will block out the noise in your hotel room

Papaya Café, Senggigi

from the nightclubs lining the main road in central Senggigi, you might as well get out there and join 'em. This unassuming place with a cute name is actually a nightclub with real *attitude*. It serves meals, and the drinks list is extensive, but most come here to rock out until midnight to the in-house band covering the latest hits in Indo-glish with commendable aplomb.
Jalan Raya Senggigi Km 8; 0370-693616

Sahara Club & Karaoke, Senggigi

Most patrons are locals, so this is a chance to meet some "Mataramians" and "Senggigites" and test your vocal chords in the karaoke bar. If you'd rather not, Indonesian DJs and FDJs (female versions) with names like DJ Bone and DJ Winky operate from (according to their billboards) "10pm to drop." The Sahara doesn't get pumping until after midnight, when the live venues like the Papaya have closed, thereby ensuring that almost no-one in Central Senggigi will get any sleep until "drop."
Jalan Raya Senggigi Km 8; 0370-6647077

SOUTHERN LOMBOK

The Shore Beach Bar, Kuta

Yep, even this little version of Kuta has something to offer after dark. Set along a surprisingly noisy part of the beach road where bars and karaoke joints noisily compete, it looks cavernous and uninviting—sort of like a country town hall. DJs strut their stuff from 9pm nightly, with live music also on Tuesday, Thursday, and Saturday nights. After closing, the party often flows over to the beach only meters away, especially during full moon. There's no dress code, of course, but you do have to wear *something*.
Jalan Parawisata Kuta; 0370-653144

BEST KID-FRIENDLY ACTIVITIES

The young 'uns will want to have some fun, too

Bali is renowned, certainly among Australians, as an ideal holiday destination for families. From adventure parks to beaches and arcades to waterslides, Bali has it all; Lombok far less so, however. But the kids may surprise you — and themselves — by becoming interested in the elegant traditional dances and chaotic public markets. In any case, the local people truly adore all kids, and yours will be admired and probably cuddled (if they're of an appropriate age).

SOUTHERN BALI

Waterbom Park, Kuta

This world-class facility superbly set among four hectares of tropical gardens has won numerous awards for its ecological sustainability and European-standard safety. Kids — and the young at heart — can whoop it up on rides like "Smashdown" and "Boomerang," while those without the need for an adrenaline rush may prefer more gentle tubing down the "Lazy River." There are also plenty of smaller slides for the pre-teenies and spots for parents to relax with a drink or snack.
Jalan Kartika (Tuban); open daily 9am–6pm; US$31/19 adults/ children (2–12); 0361-755676; waterbom-bali.com

Beachwalk, Kuta

Yes, it does rain and sometimes the kids just prefer noisy video games to gentle pony rides. Much of the third floor of the new Beachwalk shopping/entertainment complex is dedicated to kids and their long-suffering parents. There are plenty of cafés around the cutely-named "Miniapolis" for Mum and Dad to sit while pretending to watch their offspring. There's even a drop-and-shop care center and play group where parents can leave their kids for an hour or two of tantrum-free shopping. Another attraction is the only cinema complex on Bali outside of Denpasar.
Jalan Pantai Kuta; open daily 10am–12am; 0361-8464888; beachwalkbali.com

Waterbom Park, Kuta

The Bali Treetop Adventure Park, Central Highlands

Bali Horse Adventure, near Seminyak

This company—one of a few offering horse rides along the isolated beaches north of Seminyak—caters very well for children. The experienced teachers offer lessons for all ages and encourage kids to interact with the horses by grooming and preparing them. The more apprehensive can amble through the local village by *cidomo* (horse and cart), which is great fun in a group, or the smaller ones can plod along the beach on a docile pony. Parents can join in, of course, or relax at the stables knowing their loved ones are in safe hands and having a great time.

Jalan Pura Dalem Lingsir, Banjar Pengembungar; 0361-3655597; balihorseadventure.com

UBUD

Taman Burung Bali Bird Park & Rimba Reptil, Singapadu

This immaculate park spread over two hectares is home to about 1,000 birds, including Indonesian species like the elusive Bird of Paradise and endemic Bali Starling. While these are kept in aviaries, dozens of others roam free, such as toucans and macaws. The website has up-to-date information about events, interactive feeding programs and bird of prey shows. The ticket includes entrance to the Reptile Park opposite which is less impressive, though the Komodo Dragons are likely to keep the young 'uns enthralled for a while longer.

Open 9am–5.30 daily; US$26/14 adults/ children (2–12); Jalan Serma Cok Ngurah Gambir, Singapadu (between Sanur & Ubud); 0361-299352; bali-bird-park.com

Pondok Pekak

Few cultural options are available for the youngsters, but this charming library-cum-hangout does offer a range of courses that may appeal to kids, e.g., carving fruit and vegetables and creating colorful offerings, as well as other programs particularly designed for children, such as *gamelan* and dance. It also boasts a children's library (open 10am–5pm) and an upstairs reading room. Local children often come here for

Families enjoy dolphin watching along Bali's coastline.

Legong dance lessons and bilingual storytelling, so your kids can also meet others their own age. And there's a rare field of grass opposite (although, inexcusably, partially used as a car park).
Open 9am-9pm daily; east of football field, Jalan Monkey Forest; 0361-976194; librarypondok@yahoo.com

CENTRAL HIGHLANDS

Bali Treetop Adventure Park, Candikuning

Those screams you can hear in the forest are kids enjoying themselves. This educational and environmentally-friendly park has 72 activities from the 160m-long flying-fox to Tarzan jumps. Circuits are designed for different age groups from Yellow Squirrel (4-6 years old) to the Green Circuit suitable for all ages—although the Black Adrenaline Circuit where kids, according to the brochure, need "courage… to execute breathtaking jumps" could make parents white-knuckled. But there is an immense focus on training and safety, with each child attached to ropes and other gad-

gets as if they're scaling Mount Everest.
Open daily 8.30am-6pm; US$21/14 for adult/child (up to 12); Bedugul Botanical Gardens; 0361-852 0680; balitreetop.com

NUSA LEMBONGAN

Bali Hai Cruises

Want to spoil the kids and have oodles of fun yourselves, too? Bali Hai is one of a few companies that offer day trips from southern Bali on *massive* boats that dock beside even larger pontoons off the coast of Nusa Lembongan island. The kids (and you) will love the Reef Cruise with unlimited activities on and below the water, such as banana boats, snorkeling and water slides. There's a range of other activities for various age groups, like Bubble-Maker Snorkeling, as well as a supervised Kids Club. Prices may seem high, but they include hotel transfers, buffet lunch, equipment, as well as all activities.
$98/49 for adults/children (4-14) & family package (2 adults, 3 children) $275; 0361-720331; balihaicruises.com

BEST **OUTDOOR ACTIVITIES**

It's not just about shopping and eating

Encircled by sand, surf, and reefs, and with pristine forest still clinging to the volcanic interiors, it's no wonder that every conceivable outdoor activity is available on Bali and Lombok, with the exception of snow-skiing (but that's probably only a matter of time). A rash of companies has sprung up unabated in recent years, offering all sorts of activities, but to ensure maximum enjoyment and minimal problems, read this brief guide and choose a company that has earned the trust of patrons over many years.

SURFING

After the European artists of the 1930s, it was Australian surfers who then "discovered" Bali (again) during the 1960s, and the long-haired and weather-beaten have been flocking there and, more recently, Lombok, ever since. The best time on

Surfing at Kuta Beach, Bali

either island is April to October, while the best surf is along the southern coasts.

On Bali, many keep to Kuta with its predictable breaks and après-surf entertainment, as well as lessons, rental, repairs, and life-guards, so it's ideal for novices. The magical but difficult breaks around Bukit Peninsula aren't far from Kuta, though horrendous traffic has encouraged many to stay in the numerous "surfer inns" popping up like (magic) mushrooms near treasured spots such as Ulu Watu and Padang-Padang. Others such as Nyang Nyang are kept "secret" for fear of development, but currently access to most surf spots, around the peninsula is on motorbike via remote roads and down very steep steps.

Elsewhere around Bali, Nusa Lembongan is increasingly popular for its laidback charm and cheap living, but breaks are 200m (218yds) offshore (although accessible by chartered boat). Balian is also becoming fashionable among experts and untanned first-timers. Many also now flock to Lombok where the southern coast is almost one continuous wave, although access is often along deplorable roads and then by chartered boats to waves 200m (218yds) or more off shore. Facilities are still basic for surfers on Lombok — except for the surfer enclave at Gerupuk — so most day trip from Kuta where lessons, rentals, repairs and chartered boats are available. For more information, check out surfingbali.com and baliwaves.com, as well as Periplus's *Surfing Indonesia*.

SCUBA DIVING

Surrounded by colorful reefs teeming with a variety of marine life, including giant turtles and rare mola mola sunfishes, and toss in a shipwreck, and you'll understand why scuba diving is

Diving off Nusa Lembongan

big, big business these days. Outfits with swimming pools for training courses, villas for guests, and bars for après-dive gloating are sprouting up everywhere. Obviously, choose a company that's experienced, has modern equipment, is environmentally aware and recognized by PADI, the international regulator. (See the individual sections for some recommended companies.) Other matters to consider are carrying a current and recognized diving certificate; buying/renting a special camera; taking out specific diving insurance; and not overdoing it because, for example, currents can be deceptively strong.

Day trips can be arranged to any diving site from your hotel, but to save on costs and traveling times (so you can dive early and avoid the crush of tanks and flippers), consider basing yourself at these places:

1) **Padangbai**—with several easy and accessible sites, including islets at Candidasa, and day trips to Nusa Lembongan

2) **Nusa Lembongan**—with pristine reefs, as well as challenging dives with superb visibility around nearby Nusa Penida, touted as Diving's Next Big Thing

3) **Amed**—with numerous reefs, it's also close to (and a better place to stay than) Tulamben, famous for the shipwreck of the USAT Liberty Glo

4) **Gili Trawangan**—the best base from which to explore the three famed Gili Islands

5) **Lovina**—the most accessible base in northern/western Bali for the superb attractions at Pemuteran and Pulau Menjangan island

All relevant websites are operated by diving agencies, so the best source of independent information is still Periplus's *Diving Indonesia* guidebook.

SNORKELING

Those who prefer the more sedate and cheaper option of using mask, snorkel, and fins will still find plenty to please. Inevitably, the best snorkeling spots have attracted shacks that rent gear, but serious snorkelers may want to bring their own. While some of the best spots are within swimming distance of the beach, remember that seas can be cold and currents and waves often strong— and they'll be no lifeguards to rescue you. To reach the very best spots, you will need to charter a boat or join an organized tour (especially popular from the Gili Islands); costs will include rental of equipment.

Gentle offshore snorkeling (ideal for novices and children) is particularly good at Amed, Padangbai, Pasir Putih, and Nusa Lembongan, as well as the Gili Islands and Senggigi on Lombok. Stronger swimmers will enjoy the remarkable underwater delights of the famed shipwreck at Tulamben, while the magical trio of islets at Candidasa and the protected island of Pulau Menjangan are accessible by boat. Refer to the individual sections for more details, and to Periplus' *Diving Indonesia* guidebook for further independent advice.

Parasailing at Tanjung Benoa

WATER SPORTS

With plenty of coastline—and even a few volcanic lakes—a whole gamut of water sports are available. This is one of the few activities affordable for (and, therefore, popular with) Balinese visitors and Indonesian tourists, although they often settle for more sedate, family-oriented and inexpensive options like swan-shaped pedal-boats, canoes, and banana boats. Foreign tourists, especially the younger ones, may prefer more adventurous activities like parasailing, jet-skiing, wind-surfing, and water-skiing.

All of these and much more are available at four main areas where the waters are calmer: (1) Sanur, a lovely and

accessible beach, but no good during low tide; (2) Tanjung Benoa, undoubtedly the epicenter for all water activities, although it can become alarmingly busy at times; (3) Nusa Dua, but with five-star prices in line with the type of accommodation available there; and (4) the Bedugul recreation area on Lake Bratan, which has less on offer but with prices designed for locals, not foreigners. Almost no water sports are available anywhere on Lombok.

RAFTING

Not all the fun revolves around the seas and lakes. White water rafting down the rivers Ayung (more common) and Telaga Waja (more challenging) has always been popular. Rafts float along rivers fed by gushing waterfalls and through lush gorges flanked by rice terraces, but sometimes you'll spend more time hanging on for dear life than appreciating the scenery. Trips along the Ayung, for instance, can be up to 10km (6.2

miles) with about 30 rapids between Class II (fun) and Class III (exciting), and up to Class IV (adrenaline-pumping) during the wet season. While rafting is possible all year, it is more fun but volatile from November to March. Most companies are based in and around Ubud, although they will pick up guests from most hotels down south. (Therefore, if you're in Ubud ask for a discount.) Whilst on board, dress with the assumption that you'll get soaked a thousand times, and also bring a towel, change of clothes, (tight) hat, sunscreen, and solid footwear (but not flip-flops/thongs).

By using long-running and reputable agencies such as those listed below, you'll know the equipment will be up to date, insurance will be included, staff will be experienced, and there'll be welcome extras like a hot shower and meal when you finish.

- **Bali Adventure Tours** (baliadventuretours.com)—the original still has an excellent reputation
- **Bali Rafting** (balirafting.net)— cheapest rates (particularly online) but still highly-regarded
- **Sobek** (balisobek.com)—established in 1989, it's fanatical about equipment and safety

White water rafting on the Ayung River

CYCLING

The scary mountainous terrain and the even more frightening traffic are not conducive to cycling, nor are the potholed roads and maniacal truck drivers. But there are some enjoyable places to explore by pedal power, e.g., some temples around Ubud, the magnificent beach promenade at Sanur, a few villages near Lovina, the beaches of Nusa Lembongan, and the sandy paths around the Gili Islands. Bicycles can be rented at each of these locations (refer to the individual sections for details).

One popular option, and an outstanding way to increase your cultural experience while enhancing your physical wellbeing, is a half- or full-day cycling tour. These tours use back roads to pass through and stop at rice fields, temples, viewpoints, and villages — and are, importantly, designed to run downhill. A van takes you to the starting point, then carries your gear and leads the way, so all you have to do is pedal—and often just freewheel downhill. Costs will include bike, helmet, water, and (often) lunch and/or breakfast. It's an ideal family outing. Most companies are based in Ubud, but will pick you up from anywhere in the south.

Recommended companies include:
- **Bali Bike Baik Tours** (balibike. com) — committed, popular, and Balinese-owned
- **Bali Ecocycling** (baliecocycling. com) — one of the originals, it's educational and not just recreational
- **Banyan Tree Bike Tours** (banyantreebiketours.com) — great fun, informative, and finishes with a meal in a family compound

Hardier souls bringing their own mountain bikes may wish to research some possible routes on the independent fanatics' website balibybike.com.

BEST MUSEUMS & GALLERIES

Art to see and art to buy, and a little more besides

The various manifestations of Balinese art are on display everywhere and everyday around the island, but to see the best of it up close, and to give you some appreciation of quality and idea of prices, visit these art galleries (where items are for sale) and art museums (where they are not). Sadly, with one notable exception listed below, the non-art museums run by the provincial and district governments on Bali and Lombok, such as the National Museum in Denpasar, offer a disappointing collection of dusty artefacts of minimal interest. General opening times are 9am–5pm daily.

SOUTHERN BALI

Biasa Artspace, Legian

The Indonesian word *biasa* means "ordinary" but this gallery is anything but. Since 2005, it has featured works by contemporary and nonconformist artists whose creativity would not be displayed in more conventional galleries. The informative website lists the names (and features the works) of the multitude of Balinese, Indonesian, and foreign artists who are (and have been) on permanent and temporary display. Renovation is a key theme: the building was recently refurbished and is now bigger and bolder than ever, while the gallery is also involved in the restoration and conservation of art that inevitably gets affected by the tropical environment.
Jalan Raya Seminyak 34; 0361-8475766; biasaart.com

Museum Pasifika, Nusa Dua

This magnificent collection, possibly the largest of its kind in the Asia-Pacific region, is housed in an unassuming brick complex squeezed among the mega-resorts. The eleven rooms surrounded by a pleasant garden contain a myriad of sculptures, textiles, carvings, and artefacts from across Indonesia and the region. The focus is on paintings, with items from Bali and beyond, both modern and traditional, including temporary exhibits featuring foreign painters who comprised the "Ubud scene" during the 1930s. While the theme of each room is described well, it is disap-

Museum Pasifika, Nusa Dua

pointing that most exhibits are perfunctorily labelled with no detailed explanations. Inside, the café sells a limited selection of drinks and cakes.
Near Melia Bali hotel; 0361-774935; museum-pasifika.com

Ganesha Gallery, Jimbaran

You may have to squeeze past the security guard and commandeer a buggy to find it among the vast complex of villas, but this gallery is worth visiting for its small but eclectic displays of contemporary art. Often abstract but always interesting, Ganesha has held exhibitions for nearly 20 years with the aim of promoting up-and-coming Balinese and Indonesian artists, including sculptors and photographers, as well as foreign artists influenced by, and enamored with, Bali. The sound of waves crashing along the beach nearby and of birds chirping among the tropical gardens certainly adds to the experience.
Four Seasons Resort; 0361-701010

UBUD

Agung Rai Museum of Art (ARMA)

Regarded as *the* center for visual and performing arts in Ubud, ARMA is a one-stop shop for all things cultural and culinary. The five pavilions are crammed with traditional and contemporary Balinese art by renowned local masters, as well as foreigners who came to Ubud before WWII, such as the German Walter Spies, many of whom are the subject of historical portraits. Each piece of work is brightly lit and informatively labeled. The five hectares of gloriously landscaped gardens feature shady courtyards, water gardens, coffee shops, restaurants, and even some villas. And if that's not enough, ARMA offers traditional performances (see page 111) and courses in arts & crafts (see pages 108-109).
Jalan Raya Pengosekan; 0361-976659; armamuseum.com

Museum Puri Lukisan

Ubud's oldest museum was established to develop and promote Balinese art, but now also aims to preserve and document this vital industry and tradition. The three pavilions are spacious with nothing but wall-to-wall paintings and carvings, and everything is well explained and labeled. The focus is on traditional and modern works by artists inspired by Bali, such as Walter Spies and the Dutchman, Rudolf Bennet, and by masters like I Gusti Nyoman Lempad, regarded as the island's greatest. The museum also features sketches and carvings, and pictorials of the local art scene from the 1930s. (Information about workshops is on pages 108-109.)
Jalan Raya Ubud; 0361-971159; museumpurilukisan.com

Neka Art Museum

While the divine setting is similar to that found at ARMA and Puri Lukisan, this museum is often ignored because of its comparative distance, so it's far quieter. The Neka is also as much a working art shop as a museum, so you can observe artists at work; and the many seats encourage visitors to relax and relish the displays while thumbing through art books or listening to staff play *gamelan* in the courtyard. Most works are explained in detail, with a focus on the supremo I Gusti Nyoman Lempad and Ubud's influx of foreign artists before WWII. The gallery of photos of Bali from the 1930s is worth the visit alone.
Jalan Raya Sanggingan; 0361-975074; museumneka.com

Rudana Museum & Fine Art Gallery

This place is distant and rarely visited so it's more tranquil and inviting than other museums, and staff have the time and interest to show visitors around. Much of the art in the gallery is produced in Ubud and mostly contemporary, but rarely abstract. Works include charming portraits of young and old Balinese, often done with water colors, and huge canvases showcasing the grandeur of the landscape and intricacies of village life. The rooms are substantial and breezy, the gardens are enticing and the open-air workshop is usually full of artisans busily adding to the collection. The gallery (which is free to enter) is far more enticing than the museum (with a comparatively high entry charge).

Jalan Cok Rai Podok 44, Peliatan (south of Ubud); 0361-975779; therudana.org

Threads of Life

This two-roomed gallery specializes in textiles, weaving, and baskets. But what makes Threads of Life different is that all the products on sale are made by cooperatives across Bali and Indonesia with the aim of preserving traditional practices, empowering the makers (who are mostly women), and ensuring maximum profits for the producers. And what makes this gallery worth visiting are the highly informative displays about everything—whether woven cushions from Sulawesi, incense made in Bali, or traditional skirts created in Kalimantan—and the fascinating bios about the cooperatives involved, often from remote islands of the Nusa Tenggara chain, east of Bali.

Jalan Kajeng 24; 0361-972187; threadsoflife.com

CENTRAL HIGHLANDS & NORTH COAST

Museum Gunungapi Batur, Penelokan

An honourable inclusion must be made for the Volcano Museum located along the crater rim of Bali's most active *gunung api* (meaning "fire mountain" in Indonesian). Unlike any other public museum in Bali and Lombok—and, quite probably, the rest of Indonesia—this is actually interesting, spacious, well labeled and free. Spread out across two levels, the models, photos, posters, and lumps of lava help explain the history and geological evolution of Gunung Batur and its crater and lake, and of other volcanoes across the archipelago. The displays are so well-designed and informative (in good English) that you'll actually want to read about types of rocks you never knew existed and still can't pronounce.

0361-67678

GILI ISLANDS & WESTERN LOMBOK

Asmara Collection, Senggigi

It's easy to miss this two-storey shop among the nightclubs and cafés of central Senggigi. Located in front of the sophisticated courtyard restaurant of the same name, Asmara features a vast range of artefacts, souvenirs, and other items from Lombok and across the rest of the country, all at (according to stern signs inside) *fixed prices*. And, it has to be said, the prices also seem steep. But the gallery is certainly worth at the very least looking around to admire, *inter alia*, wood-carvings from Papua and ornamental *kris* daggers from Java. Or maybe buy some reasonably (fixed)-priced mementoes like perfumed soaps, ornate fans, and rattan handbags?

Jalan Raya Senggigi Km 8; 0370-693109; asmara-group.com

BEST SPAS & RETREATS

After all that shopping and rafting, you may need to relax...

Used for medical and spiritual reasons over many centuries, Balinese have now made massage an art form of commercialization. Massages on the beach are popular and convenient, but the multitudes of parlors along the back streets offer less sand, more privacy, and other treatments like facials. Further up the scale are the sophisticated "treatment centers" in Seminyak, with prices still far below those of the West, while in Ubud yoga and meditation are popular. Some visitors seek spiritual and medical treatment from *balian* traditional healers, but with one exception (listed below) they mostly work at home and won't deal with westerners because of the linguistic and cultural divide. The best online resources are balispaguide.com, and balispirit.com, which includes a list of genuine *balian* who deal with foreigners.

SOUTHERN BALI

Jari Menari, Seminyak

The name of this award-winning place — "dancing fingers" — says it all, as the male staff use the perfect amount of pressure, stretching, and rhythm, especially during the popular "four-handed massages" using two masseuses in tandem. Many treatments are influenced by yoga, while others use vibrating Tibetan "singing bowls." Also popular are the lunch-and-spa packages with Indonesian, Japanese, or Mexican themes, and training courses that impart some of their secret techniques. Bookings for anything are advised.
Jalan Raya Basangkari 47; 0361-736740; jarimenari.com

The Private Spa Wellness Center, Seminyak

The owner has fused 20 years of knowledge and experience to create something unique as it wins award after award. The personalized spa treatments and therapies use modern physiology and ancient ritu-

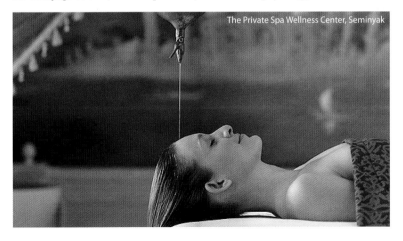

The Private Spa Wellness Center, Seminyak

Balinese traditional massage, SPA Healthland, Nusa Dua

als, while guests can also enjoy the themed rooms and Vitality Hydro Pool. Expats thrive on popular but expensive treatments such as "The Private My-Oxy Caviar De-aging" and the all-encompassing "Restore & Refresh Top to Toe Ritual."
Jalan Dhyana Pura (Camplung Tanduk) 4; 0361-731648;
privatespawellnesscenter.com

M'Spa, Seminyak
The beautiful people of Petitenget will be peeved that their secret is now more public. This all-male masseuse therapy center situated above a charming gallery offers Balinese, Swedish, Thai, and Hawaiian massages, as well as the four-handed "Meng" special — or a combination of all five. The pink-skinned may appreciate the cucumber and aloe "Sunburn Skin Journey," while other treatments use special concoctions of honey, sesame seeds, clove, and ginger, as well as Balinese *kopi* (coffee).
Jalan Laksamana 18B; 0361-736910

Desa Seni, Canggu (near Seminyak)
Desa Seni (which, oddly, means "art village") is a vast resort offering an extraordinary range of classes in yoga and meditation, as well as gym sessions,

dance lessons for the kids, and special celebrations during full moon. Monthly timetables, with helpful explanations if you don't know what the hell *vinyasa bhakti* means, are available at yoga-type places around Ubud, and online. It also publishes the very informative *Kula* magazine (also online).
Jalan Subak Sari 13, Pantai Berawa; 0361-8446392; desaseni.com

Power of Now Oasis, Sanur
This relative newcomer has secured prime beach frontage. Their busy schedule includes daily classes in Balinese and Indian yoga and meditation, and even karate, with an emphasis on family and children's activities too. If that's not enough, there's training courses, spiritual workshops, yoga-esque things for sale, and personalized healing sessions — all in an open-air thatched barn with a stall selling impossibly healthy drinks and a garden with a resident cow and hammocks.
Mertasari beach; 0878-61534535; powerofnowoasis.com

SPA Healthland, Nusa Dua
This is one of the latest to incorporate the "medical-spa" concept which involves

preventing illnesses, improving well-being, increasing lifespan, and slowing the aging process. Staffed by experts trained in the U.S., the center is a large place among larger hotel complexes. Although only opened in 2012, it's now so popular it plans to expand beyond the organic café, shop, and pharmacy.
Jalan Amphi; 0361-773565;
spahealthland.com

Home Spa, Tanjung Benoa

This place is head and shoulders (and every other part of your aching body) above the local competition. Set back from the road and tastefully designed with fountains and foliage, Home Spa offers an impressive array of enticing treatments. Maybe try the descriptive "coconut body glow," "honey lover" or "happy feet," or the more traditional "Balinese Boreh," which use spices and herbs to help relieve fever and headache. Or perhaps truly indulge yourself with the ultra-decadent "wine spa" or "chocolate body bliss."
Jalan Pratama 97; 0361-776927

Jamahal Spa, Jimbaran

Heartily recommended by many, and winner of several international awards, Jamahal is part of a gorgeous complex of villas (and is open to the public). The highly-attentive staff offer a range of treatments using organic products, including hot stone (from Polynesia) for stress and Ayurveda (from India) for "mental anguish." It pampers couples with tandem therapies, such as the "honeymoon cleansing ritual" which focusses on feet, hands, and face. The baths using green tea and the "chocolate body wrap" also sound delicious.
Jalan Ulu Watu 1; 0361-704394;
jamahal.net

UBUD

Intuitive Flow

This self-dubbed "sanctuary for yoga & healing" is housed in an ochre-colored building along a tranquil lane just up the steps from the main road. Various levels of yoga classes aimed at relaxation and mental clarity are held in classes (or privately) upstairs—no doubt, making it hard to close your eyes for meditation while wanting to admire the views. It also offers treatments for a variety of ailments, from back pain to anxiety and asthma.
Penestanan; up footpath from Jalan Raya Ubud; 0361-977 824;
intuitiveflow.com

Radiantly Alive

Tucked away in an enclave of yoga-ness and spirituality, this place offers a different range of treatments, such as Medical Qigong, an ancient method to massage internal organs, as well as personalized therapies to improve emotional, physical, and spiritual well-being. But its bread and butter (or low-cholesterol non-dairy spread) is yoga, with all sorts of classes at all sorts of levels provided every day.
Jalan Jembawan 3; 0361-978055;
radiantlyalive.com

Yoga Barn

Priding itself on its variety of programs and treatments, commitment to clients and experienced trainers, the Yoga Barn offers many types of healing therapies, but is better known for its yoga classes. Fanatics can become members, but if spiritual enhancement doesn't grab you everyone is welcome at the Monday film nights and the Little K garden café (lunch and breakfast only). The setting is delightful with laughter from the nearby

Students enjoy a yoga class at Power of Now Oasis, Sanur.

school enhancing the serenity, although current construction of a hotel next door does not.
Jalan Raya Pengosekan; 0361-971236; theyogabarn.com

Traditional Balinese Healing Center

This ramshackle shop clogged with plants and jars of herbal medicines is home to a traditional spiritual healer, unusually a young woman. She offers a range of treatments starting with a "body reading." Then you'll be rubbed and scrubbed, and later prescribed with whatever you need to improve your well-being. Packages, which are a fraction of the price charged by foreign-run places, include massage and a lunch packed with vitamins. Training courses are also offered.
Jalan Jembawan 5; 0361-8843042

Ubud Sari Health Resort

This resort arranges reasonably-priced, all-inclusive one- and two-week "Body, Mind & Spirit Rejuvenation" packages, with or without accommodation, in their tranquil villas. The general public are also welcome to try exquisite delights such as Javanese *lulur* (massage and scrub, often with green tea or strawberries), and yoga or meditation classes, or just drop by their charming vegan restaurant set above a pond.
Jalan Kajeng 35; 0361-974393; ubudsari.com

GILI ISLANDS & WESTERN LOMBOK

Club Arena Spa, The Santosa Villas & Resort, Senggigi

Like Bali's Kuta, most places around Senggigi only offer the usual array of uninspiring massages and pedicures. The best options are in the upmarket hotels, but most of these are remote—except The Santosa. Treatments range from the "Deluxe Room Treatment" (with aromatherapy massage and milk bath) to the "Refreshment Package" (which is heaven-on-a-stick for three hours). Management could make the names of the treatments a little more stimulating, but the service, facilities, and convenience cannot be faulted.
Jalan Raya Senggigi Km 8; 0370-693090, ext 1050; santosalombok.com

BEST **TOURS** & CLASSES

Learn more about crafts, food, and language, too

If you've booked a half- or full-day "tour," it'll most probably be just you and a friend or two in an air-conditioned car, which is more comfortable than a bus tour, of course, but adds to the appalling traffic. These tours are a sensible way to visit a lot of major sights within a limited time-frame, but you can easily change the itinerary—or design a different one in advance—to incorporate things that interest you and which are off the well-worn tourist trail. And this is worth considering because so few tour companies offer anything different. Otherwise, join a few classes and help improve your artistic, culinary and linguistic skills—while also having a ball.

Cultural Tours

The words "eco," "cultural," and "green" are tossed about on websites and brochures of tour companies to impress visitors, but they're rarely environmentally responsible or culturally aware. One definite exception is **JED** (0361-3669951; jed.or.id). It was established 10 years ago to provide tourists with a unique opportunity to experience village life, with the dual purpose of minimizing the ecological impact of mass tourism and maximizing profits for the community (and not some faceless entrepreneurs in Jakarta). While you can day trip to one of four associated villages, including Tenganan and on Nusa Cenginan island,

it's far more rewarding to stay overnight (but not possible in Tenganan). This means you will really get to know the villagers, and maybe attend a ceremony or help with buying and cooking food. JED is also involved in turtle conservation and release in western Bali.

If you want a guide to show you around on foot, with an emphasis on the local culture and environment, visit Topi Inn in Padangbai; ask around at homestays in regional centers like Tirtagangga and Toya Bungkah (Bali) and Tetebatu (Lombok); and in Ubud check out the bulletin boards at the Kafe and Bali Buddha cafés, and **Pondok Pekak** library.

Regional Tours

Bali and Lombok are relatively easy to get around, but the rest of the region is not, which is a very good reason to take a tour if you're visiting nearby islands.

The long-established shuttle bus company Perama (peramatour.com) also offers the popular and engaging **Hunting Komodo by Camera** tour to observe these giant prehistoric-looking lizards. The three-day trips leave Senggigi every week or so and travel by traditional (but renovated) schooner boats to Komodo Island, where you'll be

led by experienced guides with very large sticks through the jungle to witness the Komodo dragons as close as anyone dares. You then sail back to Lombok or fly from Labuhanbajo on Flores. Other highlights include an overnight stay on a remote island, visiting traditional villages, and snorkeling.

Nusa Penida, the largest island off the coast of Bali or Lombok, has plenty of attractions but is difficult to reach and even more challenging to get around. So, a tour with **CASPLA** (baliseaview.com) makes a lot of sense. They offer a choice of trips that include the eerie Gua Karang Sari cave; Pura Penataran Agung Ped temple, one of the most revered anywhere on Bali; and the sort of beaches, like Crystal Bay, that are perfect—and perfectly undeveloped (so far). They include stops at the obligatory weaving workshops, but the astounding cliff-top views may be more gratifying.

Cooking Courses

These very popular courses are offered by many companies, but visitors are sometimes disappointed with the standard of teaching and astounded that a half-day lesson can cost more than a full-day's rafting. Students wake up before the roosters and amble around a

Visitors learn woodcarving at Puri Lukisan Museum, Ubud.

village market searching for, and bargaining over, the freshest and tastiest ingredients. The trainer/chef then explains the history and process of traditional cooking as you whip up a dozen or more Indonesian and Balinese treats, such as *sayur urab* (cold mixed vegetables) and *opor ayam* (chicken cooked in coconut). Then the fun really begins as you eat what you've cooked. Better places will provide a certificate allowing you to officially try this back home and a list of recipes to help you do so. More expensive courses will also provide free pick-up around southern Bali. Two courses that are particularly recommended are:

- **Paon Bali** (paon-bali.com)—at Lalapan, near Ubud, which uses a traditional village kitchen
- **Bumbu Bali** (balifoods.com)—at Tanjung Benoa, which is the original and offers very impressive facilities

Arts & Crafts Courses

A number of places run courses from two hours to two days, and it's no surprise that the best—including these three—are in Ubud. Courses should be booked at least one day in advance.

The **Agung Rai Museum of Art**, or ARMA (armamuseum.com), offers such an enticing range of cultural programs that it's hard to choose, whether it's music (e.g., how to play the *gamelan*); woodcarving, painting, or *batik* (and the chance to actually take home your own "Balinese" souvenir); dancing (with separate classes for men and women); cooking (and even more eating); or spiritual (e.g., lectures about Hinduism).

The splendid **Puri Lukisan Museum** (museumpurilukisan.com) has the same sort of programs as ARMA, plus a few interesting alternatives, such as flute

A mask painting class at Puri Lukisan Museum, Ubud

playing and mask painting. Also, the courses here for carving and painting last all day, which is better value and allows you time to create something worth showing the folks back home. Lessons are held in a large open-air *bale* pavilion among the exquisite gardens.

Another worthwhile option is **Pondok Pekak** (0361-976194), a likable library-cum-hangout that's been offering courses for years in carving wood (and, interestingly, also carving fruit and vegetables); silver jewelry (a popular choice); and cultural activities such as *gamelan*, *Legong* dance (for the ladies), and modern or traditional Balinese painting. Some programs are particularly designed for children (see pages 94–95), while their ad hoc lessons in Indonesian language are also popular.

Language Courses

Spending a few hours learning some Balinese or Indonesian words is fun, and you will pick up useful phrases like "one more beer, please," but learning a language takes time, and courses need to be structured and taught by experts. That's why the Study Bahasa Indonesia in Bali programme run by the **Indonesia Australia Language Foundation** (IALF) —ialf.edu—is definitely (and personally) recommended. Operated with the assistance of the Australian Government, IALF runs language courses of 40 hours with an optional extra 20-hour cultural component. Its impressive headquarters is located in the dreary suburbs of Denpasar, but easily accessible by taxi from Kuta or Sanur.

BEST **DANCE PERFORMANCES**

Elegant, fierce, or funny—take your pick....

For centuries, traditional dances retold epic tales of Balinese history and religion, while music has always been a vital element of village ceremonies. As a major tourist drawcard, many of Bali's 200 known dances are being preserved, if only for commercial purposes, but some have been adapted to suit the needs of mass tourism. Many are performed in Ubud, where tickets are available at the entrance or from touts along the streets (for the same price). Performances start at about 7.30pm and last about an hour. Brochures from the Ubud tourist office have updated schedules, and the *Ubud Community* booklet is also very useful.

Baris Dance

This is performed solely by small groups of men dressed as "warriors" guarding their "king." The *baris* dance is ceremonial but energetic as performers in colorful costumes glare, pose, and stalk each other with "weapons" such as bows, arrows and traditional *kris* daggers. It's sometimes performed with *gamelan* music that sounds even more cacophonous than usual. Traditionally performed in temples, particularly around Bangli, you're more likely to see it added on to another type of dance performance.

Barong & Rangda Dance

This entertaining dance is about the eternal battle between good and evil repre-

sented by *Barong*, a cheeky part lion and part dog (played by two men), who protects the village, and *Rangda*, an evil child-eating witch. The dance is popular among locals and tourists—especially children—because there's plenty of action and the universal theme is easy to follow. Performances are renowned in Batubulan (between Sanur and Ubud), but more convenient at Pura Saren (Ubud Palace).

Gamelan Music

The word *gamelan* is used to describe the instruments that create a type of music that is synonymous with Bali (although slower, quieter versions are found in Java). A *gamelan* orchestra can include 50 instruments, including handmade xylophones with bronze discs and bowls, as well as drums, gongs, and bamboo flutes. Every village boasts at least one *gamelan* group, so you'll often hear it practiced in villages and during ceremonies, as well as accompaniment to traditional dances.

Kecak Dance

Sometimes called the "Monkey Dance" or "Fire Dance," the origins of *kecak* predate the introduction of Hinduism, but it was adapted with great success in the 1930s by westerners living in Ubud. Relating tales from the *Ramayana* epic,

A traditional *barong* performance in Ubud

Kecak dance, at Tanah Lot

up to 50 men in sarongs simulate a "trance" while they clap, shout, and chant in unison using *chak-a-chak* sounds similar to monkeys. Finishing with the spreading of coals and understandably timid attempts to fire-walk, it's powerful and hypnotic. Most dramatic locations and settings are around sunset at Tanah Lot and Ulu Watu temples.

Legong Dance

The most graceful and difficult is also the most popular. This features females, traditionally pre-pubescent but usually older in tourist-oriented dances. Their extraordinarily supple movements, particularly of their wrists and fingers, retell various stories, including that of a princess captured by a king but rescued by her brother and his army. Swathed in gold-threaded fabrics and heavily made-up, girls can spend years from the age of five learning various movements. (But some older professionals seem almost deformed from bending at impossible angles in their formative years.) Best seen in Ubud, particularly Peliatan village, Puri Taman Saraswati, and Pura Saren (Ubud Palace).

Topeng Mask Dance

This intense, ancient dance features men wearing masks called a *topeng*. Often performed at weddings and traditional ceremonies, it relates a myriad of

Balinese legends, and stories about the trials and tribulations of their kings. Some characters, particularly the clowns, wear special masks allowing them to speak and make appropriate noises. The grotesque masks and humorous actions are enjoyed by Balinese children who don't know they're also being given lessons in morals and philosophy. Best watched at the ARMA Museum, Ubud.

Wayang Kulit Shadow Puppets

Taken from the Javanese word *wayang* ("shadow") and Indonesian word *kulit* ("skin"), a series of puppets are held behind a screen by the *dalang* (puppeteer) and lit from the back to create shadows to the audience. Plots are based around the *Mahabharata* and *Ramayana* epics, so performances can be long, and the myriad of characters representing heroes and villains speak in Indonesian, Balinese, or Javanese, so it's more popular with locals than tourists. Modified versions can be enjoyed in Ubud at Oka Kartini and at Kerta Accommodation.

Lombok

Dance and music on Lombok are not based around the predominant religion of Islam, but on indigenous Sasak cultural traditions, and rarely performed for the benefit of tourists. Popular is *kendang belek*, a war dance featuring complex, hypnotic drumming. Also common is *gamelan*, but different instruments are played and the emphasis is more on drums than the metallic xylophonic instruments used on Bali. In villages, and on special occasions elsewhere (like Independence Day on 17 August), *peresehan* is performed, in which two "warriors" using sticks and shields engage in a mock "battle" that looks and sounds remarkably real.

BEST WALKS

You don't need hiking boots to get among the jungle and volcanoes

One way to see the countryside up close, and experience how most people on Bali and Lombok really live, is to walk; even among a market or along a beach, you'll experience so much more than from a car or bus. These walks are undemanding and easily accessible from major tourist centers. Some need a guide, which will increase your knowledge and enhance your experience anyway.

SOUTHERN BALI

Tuban to Petitenget

One of the best walks is also one of the most obvious: the entire length of the hedonistic southwest coast from the airport fence south of Tuban to the **Pura Petitenget** temple. A perfect time to start is about 3pm so you can plonk yourself down on a bean bag at a beachside café in Seminyak as the sun sets. Transport is available at any beach, but less so at the far southern end (Pantai Jasa), which is why it's better to finish at Seminyak or Petitenget. The most interesting section is through Tuban, reminiscent of a traditional fishing village and home to the elegant **Pura Dalem Tunon** temple. Between the airport fence and Kuta there's a delightful, shady path; from Kuta to Seminyak, it's a beachside promenade, shared with motorbikes; and then you'll need to walk along the beach to reach Petitenget.

Times 2½ hours; 1 hour between the airport fence and Kuta **Comfort** shady and flat **Eat & Drink** no shortage of places to eat and drink **Cycling** ideal, except between Seminyak and Petitenget, so use the path between the Ku De Ta turn-off (Petitenget) and Jalan Camplung Tanduk (Seminyak). See page 99 about bicycle rental.

UBUD

Campuhan Ridge

Follow signs from the turn-off to Warwick Ibah along Jalan Raya Ubud and poke about the **Puri Gunung Lebar** temple before crossing the bridge. Then it's a steepish climb up the ridge (and the only time you may be puffing). The hill is sacred and astoundingly devoid of motorbikes and bungalows; just undeveloped grassland with views down two ravines. After 30 minutes the path ends at Bangkiansidem village with craft stalls and ubiquitous sounds of bungalow construction. Then the views open up to rice fields and magical silhouettes of three volcanoes. And there's no place better to savior these views than the immaculate **Kafe Karsa**. About 15 minutes later, there's a main road and a choice: turn left and follow the windy, steep, and then busy roads back to Ubud (6km/3.7 miles) or go back and enjoy the walk again.

Times about 1 hour to Kafe Karsa **Comfort** steepish and shadeless to start, then flat **Eat & Drink** Kafe Karsa is worth the walk alone **Cycling** possible with mountain bike

Abangan

This popular walk starts at the entrance along Jalan Raya Ubud to Abangan Homestay (under the aqueduct). Initially, motorbikes share your path, but the landscape soon blossoms into *padi* fields where ducks incessantly quack to

Bird-watching in Ubud

Abangan Homestay

complain about bungalows gobbling up their feeding patches. Stalls selling wooden masks and painted eggs dissipate and butterflies soon emerge, fluttering in to fields of statuesque Balinese rice. At Gusti Ajik's *warung*, several rocky steps lead down to a path (which narrows alarmingly in places) with a steep ravine to your right and an aqueduct on your left. Later, turn right at the temple opposite the Italian restaurant and follow the lane past even better *padi* field views and finish next to the Puri Lukisan museum.

Times 1½ hours **Comfort** mostly flat and shady, except for 100m (109yds) in total where path is a 30cm (12in) wide ledge between an aqueduct and a ravine **Eat & Drink** several cafés **Cycling** possible, but note narrow sections and steps

Bali Bird Walk (with guide)

The jovial *Ibu* Su has been guiding twitchers across the back fields of Ubud for many years. She meets guests at the recommended Murni's Warung, and provides binoculars and instructions. Bird-spotting starts immediately, although peering into the sky while trying to avoid missing manhole covers is fraught with danger. Soon enough,

however, you're among *padi* fields busily spotting some of the 50 possible species, including the White-Bellied Swift, which has two brains so it can eat while sleeping(!), and the Javan Munia, endemic to Java and Bali. But it's not all ornithological: Su explains the extraordinary *subak* irrigation system for rice-farming and indicates plants used for medicinal and culinary purposes—all while listening out for the screeches of the Golden-Headed Cisticola. Halfway along, a farmer slices open a juicy coconut and laughs while you spill half the contents down your shirt.
0361-975009; balibirdwalk.com

Times 4 hours with plenty of stops **Comfort** flat and shady, but some narrow ledges **Eat & Drink** a few simple cafés; includes lunch at Murni's Warung

EASTERN BALI
Putung to Manggis

One of Bali's worst roads has been recently paved, so it's now far easier on the knees. And another benefit is that the start and finish are accessible by *bemo*. Begin at the junction with the warrior statue that leads to Wates Kangin village (which also merges with Duda Timur

Mount Agung, Eastern Bali

the immediate area. Also, **Genta Bali** (0363-22436), a café opposite the palace entrance, arranges hikes of two, four, or six hours around rice fields and traditional villages where the rare Hindu caste systems still function. The more adventurous may choose a guided hike (six hours) from Tenganan, a traditional Bali Aga village, to Tirtagangga through verdant forests around Bebandem and Budakeling. **Bungbung** is another agency with a tiny office attached to Hotel Rijasa (0363-21873). It organizes local hikes, as well as less strenuous downhill trips by bicycle.

and Putung). There are some uphill bits for the first 1.6km (1 mile) before the unexpected Bukit Putung **restaurant**, which offers simple meals and outstanding views. (If only the restaurant was at the *end* of the walk instead.) Then it's all downhill, with endless **views** of the east coast stretching from Padangbai to Ujung. The road eventually flattens out in Manggis, before reaching the highway between Padangbai and Candidasa.

> **Getting There** to start, take a *bemo* between Amlapura and Rendang to the turn-off; from Manggis, *bemo* and buses go to Candidasa, Padangbai, and Amlapura **Time** 2 hours (8.4km/ 5.2 miles) **Comfort** shady, though some steep parts downhill **Eat & Drink** a few simple stalls sell water **Cycling** perfect, though steep—but how to get your bike to the start?

Tirtagangga (with guide)

One region that's just *begging* to be explored on foot is the gentle rice-terraced slopes between Seraya and Agung mountains around Tirtagangga, home to Bali's best water palace. Surprisingly, hiking and trekking are not big business here, but can be arranged through any guesthouse in

NORTHERN BALI

Banjar

The best way to explore this charming village is on foot, but your legs will be grateful if you do it this way. From Lovina, take a *bemo* to the turn-off (opposite Alfa Mart) to Pedawa and an *ojek* (motorbike taxi) to the **monastery**. After wandering about there, admire the coastal **views** while walking down 1.2km (0.74 miles) to the obvious turn-off to *air panas* (hot springs) and another 600m (656yds) to the **market**. After nosing about there, turn left and follow the signs for another 1km (0.62 miles)—with one steep section—past the **Pura Desa** temple and some rare **vineyards**. After wallowing in the **hot water springs**, it's an easy 2km (1.2 miles) walk back down to the main road for Lovina via *padi* field **views**.

> **Time** 3–4 hours, including time at the monastery and springs **Comfort** to avoid crowds at the springs and to visit the morning market, start between 7am and 8am **Eat & Drink** nice café overlooks the springs **Cycling** possible to Banjar along a busy road and to the hot springs, but too steep to the monastery

Mount Rinjani, Lombok

NORTHERN LOMBOK & GUNUNG RINJANI

Senaru

From the Pondok Senaru homestay, an obvious path (10 minutes) leads down some steep steps to **Air Terjun Sindang Gila**. (Note: it has several other similar spellings.) You'll be mightily impressed with these waterfalls, but wait... there's more. Even better is **Air Terjun Tiu Kelep**, a flat 30-minute walk further upstream. Turn left at the first obvious (but unsigned) turn-off on the way back up from Sindang Gila and follow the path which crosses a "bridge" (really an aqueduct with gaping holes) and parallels a canal. Before the path ends at the river, look for another trail to your left. The turn-off is easy to miss, however, so take a guide (even a kid) from Sindang Gila or follow a local who knows. Another path (unsigned but obvious) further up from Sindang Gila and to the right follows the lip of a ridge past extraordinary irrigation tunnels with dramatic views of the falls and valleys below.

Time 1½ hours, plus time at both falls **Comfort** steepish to Sindang Gila **Eat & Drink** stalls sell water at Sindang Gila

Tetebatu (with guide)

There are endless rice fields and views of the Rinjani volcano, but even more stimulating is observing the subsistence lifestyle of locals also growing tobacco, vanilla, coffee, and chilies. The narrow "paths"—designed for nimble-footed rice farmers, and often barely ½-meter wide and muddy—continue alongside irrigation canals, across terraced *padi* fields, and through village compounds. After two hours, you're sharing a forest with lizards and butterflies, and 30 minutes later you're at the National Park HQ. From there, a paved trail (1.6km/1 mile) leads to the mighty **Air Terjun Jeruk Manis** waterfalls. The return leg starts at the access road to the park, but inevitably detours through more fields of palm trees and rice stalks. Any guesthouse, café or self-dubbed "trekking agency" along the two streets in Tetebatu can arrange a guide.

Time 4–5 hours **Comfort** shady but sweaty—the path is always narrow and often slippery **Eat & Drink** welcome kiosk at the Park HQ

TRAVEL FACTS

Bali and, to a lesser extent, Lombok are well set up for tourism, and most workers in the tourist areas speak English and have a good idea what westerners need and want. But there are some things you should know before you visit and others to keep in mind while staying on either island. Indonesia is a developing country, and some parts of Bali and Lombok remain poor and undeveloped for tourism, but you shouldn't encounter too many problems as long as you act sensibly, plan ahead, and read through this guide.

Health & Safety

While memories of the terrorist attacks on Bali in 2002 and 2005 may still be vivid for some, in reality Bali and Lombok are no more (and probably less) dangerous than your own country. Much of the infrequent crime is opportunistic (e.g., bag-snatching) and many of the dangers encountered by visitors (e.g. motorbike accidents and drowning) are caused by recklessness, often induced by alcohol, and ignoring signs and regulations. Bali and Lombok are healthy enough places, although you should take the usual precautions (e.g., bottled water and sunscreen). It's a cliché, but Bali Belly does happen. Nine times out of ten, it's your stomach adjusting to cooking oils and spices and it doesn't mean the food is unsafe. Rest up and let your body run its natural course, and avoid anti-diarrhoeal medicines, which sometimes make matters worse. No vaccinations are required. Major diseases such as malaria are very rare (but a little more common in the rural areas of Lombok). However, rabies from the numerous stray dogs and dengue fever are not uncommon. International-standard private hospitals, doctors and dentists can be found in major tourist centers. Emergency numbers on both islands are: 118 (ambulance); 110 (police); 751111 (search & rescue); and 113 (fire).

Best Time to Go

The climate (see page 4) shouldn't really affect your decision about when to travel, but the peak seasons may: July and August (when Europeans flock) and mid December to late January (Australian school holidays). At these times, the southern beaches of Bali, Nusa Lembongan, the Gili Islands and, to a lesser extent, Senggigi seem to be bursting, so accommodation is heavily booked and hotel prices often double. If you have a choice, visit in April, May, June, September, or October, or consider staying along the eastern or northern coasts of Bali, or southern Lombok.

Events

Here are a few annual events worth attending:

- Bali Spirit Festival (balispiritfestival. com)—Ubud; March; yoga, concerts & workshops
- Bali Arts Festival (baliartsfestival. com)—Denah Taman Budaya arts center, Denpasar; mid-June to mid-July; dance, music and handicrafts
- Senggigi Festival (thelombokguide. com)—July; Sasak culture and art
- Kuta Karnival (kutakarnival.com) —September; dance, competitions & parties
- Bali Palaces Festival (palacesofbali. com)—September and October; cultural activities in lesser-known palaces and temples
- Ubud Writers & Readers Festival (ubudwritersfestival.com)—October; guest authors, workshops and music

Balinese festivals are based on the unique Wuku 210-day calendar. The largest, **Galungan**, wildly celebrates the victory of good (*dharma*) over evil (*adharma*) for 10 days. This is a time when streets are brightly decorated with *penjor* bamboo poles, ceremonies are held in temples across the island, and boys in traditional outfits carry a *barong* (mock lion-dog) around the streets seeking donations. Celebrations culminate with **Kuningan**, when the Gods return to the skies.

One festival that does impact on visitors is **Nyepi** (March or April), when the entire island literally shuts down for 24 hours of reflection and sacrifice, which includes tourists who aren't permitted to leave their accommodation. Police ensure that only ambulances are allowed on the streets; *everything* else (including the airport) closes, although your hotel will remain open and staff will arrange meals. While this may seem inconvenient, the days before and after are great fun with firecrackers and giant effigies called *ogoh-ogoh* paraded along the streets and then ceremoniously burnt.

Most people on **Lombok** are Muslims who celebrate the usual **Islamic festivals** and holidays, but these are rarely open to or interesting for tourists. In the holy month of **Ramadan**, some restaurants may shut during the day or close entirely for the whole month, but there'll be no shortage of places to eat and drink in the tourist areas. During Idul Fitri, which lasts several days at the end of Ramadan, transport to, from, and across Lombok may be very busy. One popular festival worth attending is **Bau Nyale**, held in and around Kuta (Lombok) in February or March. It's a bizarre tradition where thousands from across Lombok gather to catch sea-worms, which are an aphrodisiac and sign of a bountiful harvest. Another is the "**Rice Cake War**" held at Pura Lingsar, near Mataram (see page 27), part of the Hindu **Pujawali** festival (late November or early December).

Ceremonies & Temple Etiquette

You'll almost certainly stumble across a religious ceremony at a temple, particularly Goa Lawah, Pura Besakih, and Tanah Lot, or even witness worshippers in full ceremonial costumes marching en masse along the chaotic streets of Kuta. If not, look out for signs stating *hati-hati ada upacara agama* ("be care-

ful, there's a religious ceremony") or ask locals. Tourists are welcome to watch ceremonies but not *attend* unless specifically invited; and if so, you'll need to wear the appropriate ceremonial attire.

When visiting temples, you'll need to wear a sarong (certainly if your knees or shoulders are bare) and a sash as a sign of respect. (Both are available to borrow/rent at major temples.) And some other rules: never walk in front of anyone praying or position yourself higher than a priest, and always remain quiet and distant. Pregnant and menstruating women are forbidden to enter temples because they're deemed to be spiritually unclean. Some temples are only accessible to Hindus, although this is often waived if you're accompanied by a guide.

Lombok is mainly Islamic. While Muslims rarely hold ceremonies like the Balinese Hindus, tourists are welcome to visit mosques if dressed appropriately (i.e., no short trousers/dresses or singlets, and headscarves for ladies) and behave acceptably (which includes taking off shoes). The exception is during prayers, especially on Friday; if in doubt, check with a local.

Visas

Visitors from most countries to Indonesia are issued 30-day visas on arrival. These cost US$25, but can be paid using Australian or Canadian dollars, Indonesian *rupiah*, Euros, or 12 other major European and Asian currencies. But remember: some airlines (especially in Australia) won't allow you on a flight to Indonesia unless you have a return or onward ticket within 30 days; and the day of arrival and departure are included in those 30 days.

To stay in Indonesia longer, you have three options: (1) apply for a 60 day

tourist visa (US$60) at an Indonesian embassy before departure; (2) extend your 30 day visa (once only) by another 30 days at an immigration office or, better, through a local visa agency: or (3) do the common "visa run," i.e., fly to Singapore for the day and receive another 30 day visa on return.

Money

The national **currency** is the Indonesian *rupiah* (*roo-PEE-ah*), often abbreviated to Rp or IDR. The pinkish-purply Rp10000 note (with two color variations) and the purply-pinkish Rp100000 note are similarly colored—and notice the confusing lack of commas between the appropriate zeros. Break large notes whenever possible at hotels and larger stores, and always keep wads of small change. By law, all payments must be made in *rupiah*, even if prices for upmarket hotels and tours are quoted in US$ or other foreign currencies.

Frustratingly, many upmarket restaurants and hotels don't include the compulsory 10 percent government **tax** on their menus/tariffs, but put them later on the bill, while also adding an unofficial "service charge" of 5 percent to 11 percent. (Collectively, the two taxes are

known as "plus plus.") If a service charge is added, no **tip** is needed; if not, rounding up to the nearest Rp5000 is always appreciated by underpaid staff. Tipping is not normal, but if you want to reward someone Rp5000–10,000 is enough.

Indonesians have taken to automatic teller machines (**ATMs**) like ducks to a rice field of bugs, so they (ATMs, not ducks) can be found in all tourist areas and larger towns. But to avoid inevitable (and often hefty) transaction fees, bring **cash**, which can be changed in all tourist areas (less commonly in smaller towns).

Always use banks or licensed money-changers rather than shops; check if a commission is charged (it shouldn't be); and triple-check the wad of rupiah you're given. The same goes for changing old-fashioned **travelers cheques**. Major **credit cards** are only viable in department stores and better hotels, restaurants and travel agencies, but a surcharge of 3–5 percent will probably be added.

Bargaining is expected and happily encouraged by vendors in stalls and markets. Seasoned hagglers start with a price about a third of that initially offered by the vendor, with anything from 40–60 percent of the initial offer usually acceptable by both sides. And remember:

there's no such thing as a "right price"; if the buyer and seller are both happy, then the price is "right." In supermarkets, mini-marts, and department stores where prices are marked, bargaining is bad form. Accommodation prices are almost always negotiable, but food in restaurants is not.

Time
Bali and Lombok are 8 hours ahead of Greenwich Mean Time; the same as Western Australia, Singapore, and all of Malaysia. Both islands use Central Indonesian Time (WIT), which is one hour ahead of Java. There is no daylight saving anywhere in Indonesia.

Electricity
Bali and Lombok use the 220 volt system. Plugs are the two-round pin variety used in Western Europe. Blackouts are not uncommon throughout Lombok and in rural areas of Bali, particularly where demand can be high, e.g., the Gili Islands.

Mobile Phones
To avoid a horrific bill when you return, check the costs of global roaming with your phone company before using your mobile phone in Indonesia. If you intend making many local calls, buy a pre-paid SIM card from a mini-mart for your phone or buy a local phone and SIM card. Costs are so cheap that even market traders chat on their handphones.

Internet
Many bars, restaurants, and cafés in the tourist areas offer free Wi-Fi, but it's rare elsewhere. While "free Wi-Fi" signs are common at hotel entrances, access is often limited to the reception or hotel restaurant because routers haven't been

positioned to connect the rooms. A few Internet centers have survived the smartphone revolution, although connections can still be slow. If you're staying a few weeks and need constant access, buy a prepaid modem that plugs into a USB port in your laptop. You'll be charged by the byte (not by time), so if you're just emailing and not downloading movies costs are low.

Websites
Official government tourist websites (such as tourism.baliprov.go.id) are disappointing, while others may seem helpful but are run by companies pushing their own businesses. Instead, check out these useful and (mostly) independent sites:
- balieats.com—searches, reviews and explanations
- bali-paradise.com—business, travel information and links
- baliblog.com—articles, advice and reviews
- balitravelforum.com—visitors and expats share experiences
- thelombokguide.com—online version of the essential guide for Lombok

Media
No locally-produced English-language TV or radio station is worth bothering about, but worthwhile **magazines** and **newspapers** are available in the tourist areas of Bali (but not Lombok). The *Bali Post* (balipost.co.id) is available free in a four-page format or as a wrap-around attached to the old-fashioned *Jakarta Post*. For a stimulating and opinionated read, grab the *Bali Advertiser* (baliadvertiser.biz). For events and functions, the monthly *Bali Plus* (baliplus.com) is free and pocket-sized; *The Mag* is a free monthly with a section on the Gili

Islands; and *Ubud Life* is an informative, free quarterly with interesting articles about culture. The following glossy magazines aren't free but are often available for browsing in upmarket hotels and restaurants: *The Yak* (theyakmag.com), dedicated to Seminyak; *Bali & Beyond* (baliandbeyond.co.id); and *Now!* (now-bali.co.id). For Lombok, the best (and only) is the informative bi-weekly *The Lombok Guide* (thelombokguide.com).

Arriving

PLANE Most travelers to **Bali** arrive at the only airport Ngurah Rai (ngurahrai-airport.co.id), usually simplified to "Denpasar" (DPS). Located only minutes from Kuta, a new terminal has been built at the airport and became operational in late 2013. If you've pre-booked a packaged tour, your hotel should pick you up; if not, only pay for a hotel transfer if you're staying in a remote area that taxis don't know or won't go. Immediately outside the arrivals area of both the domestic and international terminals, which are within a few minutes' walk, official taxi counters sell set-priced vouchers to all destinations. Ignore taxi touts. There's no public transport, and the Perama shuttle bus can drop you off but isn't allowed any pick-ups.

The brand spanking new Bandara Internasional Lombok (BIL) airport for **Lombok** has moved to Praya, which is handy for Kuta beach but not for the Gili islands or Senggigi anymore. (Code-named LOP, the airport is still also confusingly called both "Mataram" and "Praya.") Official taxis loiter outside the arrivals area and use meters, and are cheaper than touts with private cars. Irregular DAMRI buses link with the Sweta (Mandalika) terminal in Mataram,

and shuttle buses from tourist areas drop off passengers but won't pick up any.

DEPARTURE TAXES The Indonesian Government will slug you on arrival for visas and will hit you again upon leaving. Departure tax is not included in your ticket but payable after checking in at the airport on Bali and Lombok. The taxes for international flights from Bali/Lombok are Rp150,000/Rp100,000, and Rp50,000/Rp25,000 for domestic connections. And remember: you must pay in *rupiah*.

BOAT Hardier travelers may arrive in Bali or Lombok by boat. From Java and Sumbawa, direct buses hurtle to Denpasar, Singaraja, and Mataram using the ferry. The national ferry carrier, Pelni (pelni.co.id), connects Bali and Lombok to the rest of the archipelago through Pelabuhan Benoa harbor (near Sanur) in Bali and Lembar on Lombok every few days. Ferries also link Lembar (Lombok) and Padangbai (Bali) every 60–90 minutes; this trip takes 4–6 hours and can be uncomfortable even in calm weather. From Labuhan Lombok, ferries head every hour to Labuhan Tano on Sumbawa. A better option is Perama (peramatour.com), which offers services between the tourist areas on Bali and Lombok using the ferry and shuttle buses to/from both ports. If you're only bound for the Gili Islands, you don't even need to step foot on Lombok (see page 62).

Getting Around

PUBLIC TRANSPORT On both islands small buses and vans (often generically called *bemo*) connect main urban areas, but they're designed for the benefit of locals (especially school children and market-traders in the mornings) and not tourists. So there is, for example, limited public transport to/from Ubud, nothing to/from Amed, and you'd have to change *bemo* five times (twice in Denpasar) to travel between Padangbai and Lovina. It's cheap and a fun way to meet locals, but uncomfortable and painfully slow.

Major transport hubs on **Bali** are Semarapura and Amlapura (for the east); Singaraja (for the north); and Denpasar, which has four main terminals with services heading in all directions across Bali and Indonesia. A *bemo* can be chartered, and will take detours, for negotiable rates.

On **Lombok**, *bemo* (which are more likely to be newer pick-up trucks) are frequent along the main roads (including Senggigi), but far less so in Kuta and Tetebatu (except on market days). The transport hubs/terminals are Kebun Roek (Ampenan) in Mataram for Senggigi; Sweta (Mandalika) in Mataram for Tetebatu and Praya; Bangsal for the Gili islands; and Praya for Kuta. But you are better off using shuttle buses if available.

SHUTTLE BUSES Far more popular and comfortable are the mini-buses designed and priced for foreign tourists. On **Bali**, air-conditioned shuttle buses travel to/from (and stop anywhere along the way) Sanur, Kuta, Ubud, Padangbai, Lovina, Candidasa, Candikuning, and the airport (for drop off, not pick up). Although more expensive than public transport, the small extra cost (by western standards) is certainly worth it. Perama (peramatour.com) offers the most services, although other companies also provide shuttle buses from Ubud, Sanur and Padangbai. For other areas (e.g., Amed and Tulamben), shuttle bus agencies need a minimum of two, so it's often

cheaper (and more flexible) to charter a *bemo* or car with a driver instead. Tickets are available from travel agencies, hotels, and Perama offices.

On **Lombok**, services are less widespread and frequent. Perama links Senggigi with Bangsal (for the Gilis) and Lombok's Kuta, and will travel to Tetebatu with a minimum of two. Other agencies offer "shuttle buses" but they're often shared cars (and still preferable to public transport). Any shuttle bus ticket from Bali to Lombok (or vice versa) will almost certainly use the public ferry.

TAXIS Every second vehicle in the **Bali** resort areas of Kuta/Legian and Sanur seems to be a taxi. They're all official, metered, air-conditioned, and (almost always) driven by honest, helpful, and English-speaking drivers. Fares are set and not negotiable. Taxis are also easy to find in Nusa Dua, Tanjung Benoa, and Denpasar, but rare anywhere else on Bukit Peninsula, except Jimbaran during the popular sunset dinners. Metered taxis are allowed to drop off (but not pick up) passengers in Ubud, and are, remarkably, not available *anywhere* else on Bali.

On **Lombok**, metered taxis can only be found in Mataram, at the airport, and along the main road through Senggigi.

CHARTERING CARS & MOTORBIKES Where there are no taxis you may have to charter a car with a driver. These vehicles, which are usually modern, air-conditioned and can carry up to six passengers, are also cost-effective alternatives to taxis and shuttle buses if you're in a small group. Rates are negotiable; about Rp70,000 per hour or Rp250,000/ Rp400,000 for 6/12 hours is reasonable. Drivers hang around every corner in

every tourist center touting for business, while some even have websites and can be pre-booked online. Costs should include petrol, although you'll be obliged to pay for the driver's food, and for accommodation if you travel overnight.

At most corners in most towns and at all turn-offs in the countryside men sit patiently on or around their **motorbikes**. They are an *ojek* (motorbike taxi), offering rides on the back of their bikes to anywhere you want for any fare you're willing to pay. They're quicker and cheaper than taxis (and even carry backpacks), but a little scary for the uninitiated.

RENTING CARS & MOTORBIKES Before you even consider renting a car please mull over these realities: traffic is appalling (especially in southern Bali and Ubud); roads are often narrow, windy, and rarely signposted; and in the event of an accident you'll be responsible for compensation and repairs regardless of who is to blame. To avoid these serious issues—and to ensure you don't spend most of

your precious time getting lost, swearing at traffic, staring at maps and looking for parking spaces—charter a car with a driver. This allows you to relax and enjoy the scenery, and the driver will probably know about local ceremonies, offer explanations and take you to viewpoints not listed in any guidebook or map.

If you're still determined to rent a car yourself, vehicles are available at major tourist centers on Bali, but far less so on Lombok. This is best done through a large, reputable local travel agency; international companies, such as Avis and Budget, are poorly represented. You'll need to carry an International Licence, read the fine print of your rental agreement (which may be in "Indoglish"), and bring a bucket-full of patience. Make sure the registration papers are in the car, be aware of the insurance loopholes, and triple-check (or, better, photograph) all pre-existing scratches and dents. Rates start from Rp250,000 per 24 hours, including insurance but not petrol. Good luck.

A popular (but potentially more dangerous) option that does open up far more of the countryside is renting a motorbike. This can be arranged anywhere tourists can be found. If you can't find a travel agency offering rental, ask at your hotel; someone will rent out their bike. Rates are about Rp50,000 per day for a modest 100–125cc model. Officially, you need an International Motorbike Licence, but no-one will ever ask to see it, except for canny traffic policemen. (If caught, an on-the-spot "fine" of Rp50,000 usually keeps the cop happy, but be careful because bribery is, of course, illegal.) Helmet(s) are compulsory and will be provided, but often no more useful than wearing a tin cup. And please note: insurance is almost never included, so you'll have to pay up big-time if the motorbike is damaged or stolen; and most travel insurance policies do not cover motorbike accidents.

CYCLING Despite the traffic-clogged roads and mountainous landscapes, there are a few places where you can rent bicycles and really enjoy the fresh air and marvellous scenery. (See page 99 for more information.)

Basic Indonesian

selamat pagi	good morning
selamat siang/sore	good (early/late) afternoon
selamat malam	good evening
selamat datang	welcome
sampai jumpa (lagi)	until we meet (again)
(Ba)pak/(I)bu	Father/Mother
Apa kabar? Baik	How are you? Fine
ya/tidak	yes/no
tolong/terima kasih	please/thank you
sama-sama	you're welcome
Di mana…?	Where is…?
Berapa…?	How much/many…?
mahal/murah	expensive/cheap
Saya (tidak) mengerti	I (don't) understand
Saya mau pergi/beli…	I want to go/buy…
Pelan-pelan!	Slowly!

Glossary

air panas	hot springs
bahasa	language; so "Indonesian language" is *Bahasa Indonesia*
bale	open-air pavilion often used for meetings
bemo	generic term for public transport
danau	lake
gunung	mountain
homestay	simple family-run hotel; other terms are *losmen* and *pondok*
ikat	a woven fabric designed with special dyes
jalan	lane/road
jukung	outrigger boat used for fishing
meru	temple shrine with many thatched roofs
nasi	cooked rice
nusa	island (also *pulau*)
ojek	motorbike taxi (i.e., you're the pillion passenger)
padi	unharvested rice
pasar	market
pulau	island (also *nusa*)
pura	Balinese Hindu temple
puri	palace
rupiah	the national currency
Sasak	indigenous people of Lombok
subak	communal irrigation system for cultivating rice
taman	garden or park
warung	stall, usually selling food

INDEX

INDEX

PHOTO CREDITS

123rtf.com: thoron77 (p. 96)

Balihaicruises (balihaicruises.com): pp. 57 top, 70

Botanic Garden in Ubud (botanicgarden-bali.com): p. 45 left

Chez Gado Gado, Seminyak (gadogadorestaurant.com): pp.70 (middle), 81

Dreamstime: Anasztazia (p. 22 bottom); Dima266f (p. 19); Dimaberkut (front cover, pp. 7, 30 top, 31); Djmattaar (back cover, p. 97); Efired (p. 12); Febriyanta (pp. 3, 13); Joyful (p. 9); Magicinfoto (p. 110); Manamana (back cover, bottom left); Masterlu (front cover, bottom right & main photo, pp. 5, 45 right); Master2 (p. 27 top); Milonk (p. 28); Moth (p. 4); Mrsbeaver (p. 18); Paop (p. 66); Iryna Rasko (back cover, top right; p. 71 middle); Rchphoto (p. 24 bottom); Sintez (p. 54); Surz01 (pp. 71 top, 99); Tanhi84 (p. 115); Thoron (p. 61); Toonman (title page, p. 17 bottom); Trubavin (front cover, bottom left, pp. 30 bottom, 71 bottom right); Viviann g (p. 26); Willysetia (p. 5 top); Witthayap (front cover, top right; p. 53 top); Yuum (p. 114); Zhu_zhu (p. 111)

iStockphoto: georgeclerk (p. 55); Jacus (p. 95); JurgaR (p. 31); Robas (p. 64); lianglow (p. 65)Witthaya (p. 50)

Jazz Bar & Grille, Sanur: p. 91

Komaneka at Tanggayuda, Ubud (komaneka.com): front cover, top left; pp. 70 top right, 77

Kuta Horses (horseridinglombok.com): p. 25 bottom

Museum Pastifika, Nusa Dua (museumpasifika.com): p. 100

Papaya Café, Senggigi: p. 92

Paul Greenway (author): pp. 2, 5 bottom, 10, 11 (2 photos), 14, 15, 16, 17 top, 20, 21 (2 photos), 22 top, 23, 25 top, 26 top, 27 bottom, 29, 30 (Monkey Forest & rice fields), 32, 37, 39 (2 photos), 42, 46, 47, 50, 53 bottom, 55 bottom, 56, 57 bottom, 58, 59, 62, 63, 67 (2 photos), 69, 70 (artist and kids on rope bridge), 74, 78, 83, 85, 87, 88, 89, 94, 98, 107, 108, 109, 113 (2 photos), 116 (2 photos), 119, 123

Power of Now Oasis, Sanur (powerofnowoasis.com): p. 106

Private Spa Wellness Center, Seminyak (privatespawellnesscenter.com): p. 103

Shutterstock: Aleksandar Todorovic (p. 68); Daniel_Dash (p. 44); deepblue-photographer (p. 38); Dudarev Mikhail (pp. 3 middle, 93); Tuomas Lehtinen (p. 43)

SPA Healthland, Nusa Dua (spahealthland.com): p. 104

The Laguna Resort & Spa, Nusa Dua (thelagunabali.com): p. 75

The Oberoi, Lombok (oberoihotels.com): p. 79

The Tuttle Story: "Books to Span the East and West"

Many people are surprised when they learn that the world's largest publisher of books on Asia had its humble beginnings in the tiny American state of Vermont. The company's founder, Charles Tuttle, came from a New England family steeped in publishing.

Tuttle's father was a noted antiquarian dealer in Rutland, Vermont. Young Tuttle honed his knowledge of the trade working in the family bookstore, and later in the rare books section of Columbia University Library. His passion for beautiful books — old and new — never wavered through his long career as a bookseller and publisher.

After graduating from Harvard, Tuttle enlisted in the military and in 1945 was sent to Tokyo to work on General Douglas MacArthur's staff. He was tasked with helping to revive the Japanese publishing industry, which had been utterly devastated by the war. When his tour of duty was completed, he left the military, married a talented and beautiful singer, Reiko Chiba, and in 1948 began several successful business ventures.

To his astonishment, Tuttle discovered that postwar Tokyo was actually a book-lover's paradise. He befriended dealers in the Kanda district and began supplying rare Japanese editions to American libraries. He also imported American books to sell to the thousands of GIs stationed in Japan. By 1949, Tuttle's business was thriving, and he opened Tokyo's very first English-language bookstore in the Takashimaya Department Store in Ginza, to great success. Two years later, he began publishing books to fulfill the growing interest of foreigners in all things Asian.

Though a westerner, Tuttle was hugely instrumental in bringing a knowledge of Japan and Asia to a world hungry for information about the East. By the time of his death in 1993, he had published over 6,000 books on Asian culture, history and art — a legacy honored by Emperor Hirohito in 1983 with the "Order of the Sacred Treasure," the highest honor Japan can bestow upon a non-Japanese.

The Tuttle company today maintains an active backlist of some 1,500 titles, many of which have been continuously in print since the 1950s and 1960s — a great testament to Charles Tuttle's skill as a publisher. More than 60 years after its founding, Tuttle Publishing is more active today than at any time in its history, still inspired by Charles Tuttle's core mission — to publish fine books to span the East and West and provide a greater understanding of each.

Also available from Tuttle Publishing & Periplus Editions

tuttlepublishing.com

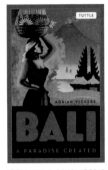

ISBN 978-0-8048-4260-0

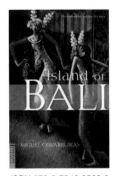

ISBN 978-0-7946-0562-9

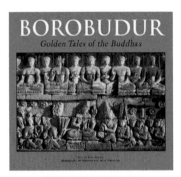

ISBN 978-0-945971-90-0

ISBN 978-0-8048-4212-9

ISBN 978-0-8048-3896-2

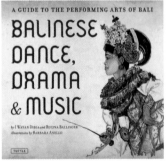

ISBN 978-0-8048-4183-2

ISBN 978-0-8048-4246-4

ISBN 978-0-8048-4198-6

ISBN 978-0-8048-4145-0